Curated by NATASHA GILMOUR and SIAN YEWD...

# THIS I KNOW IS TRUE

A collection of stories celebrating awakened
women to inspire community progress

the kind press

Cover design: Nada Backovic
Internal design: Nicola Matthews, Nikki Jane Design
Edited by: Georgia Jordan

Cataloguing-in-Publication entry is available from the National Library Australia.

NATIONAL
LIBRARY
OF AUSTRALIA

ISBN: 978-0-6450887-4-8 (Paperback)
ISBN: 978-0-6450887-5-5 (ebook)

*For all who dream of illuminating the world,*
*this ones for you, may we dance!*

# Contents

# Sunrise

*As the sun rises may we all be blessed by all our Ancestors, as we all walk together on sacred land.*

*Let's walk, grow and dream together and nurture Mother Earth, her lands, waterways and all living beings.*

*May we all make deep connections to our own Spirit, each other and continue to tell the stories that need to be told.*

*Let us all dream for truth, harmony, and healing, so we can transcend harm and create a better world.*

— Annabelle Sharman

# Acknowledgement

In unity, we acknowledge the traditional owners and all the custodians caring for the land and waterways in which we live, work, and journey. We pay respect to Elders past, present and emerging and acknowledge that sovereignty was never ceded.

# Introduction

In times of uncertainty and change, we are compelled to reach for certitudes. Something to attach to when so much is shifting around and within us. This book is an invitation to become curious about the blurred lines of reality we face in today's new world, where a particular truth is coming from and to help navigate this moment, to be able to locate your own truths. Despite feeling alone on her journey as 'one woman', this book showcases that in fact, we can all reveal our greatest light—true self. No matter who you are.

*This I Know Is True* is a collection of 18 stories, a narrative of effusive acceptance, each story a celebrated chink written with kindness and awareness.

It is good to have many stories, to collect them as we go along in life, through stories we can collectively shape our lives in mysterious ways. You deserve to take up space, to choose your path and walk with grace and confidence and truth.

Enjoy the stories, whatever season you are in, may this book be a place you can pause, catch your breath, and find inspiration.

And remember, with every sunrise, allow yourself to become someone new again, it's happening anyway.

Natasha & Sian

# 1.

# A Mutti Mutti Bush Woman's truth

## ANNABELLE SHARMAN

As I sit in Mutti Mutti Country, I ask Ancestors to guide me to story, to remind me what I know is true.

All I seem to hear as I take in this mesmerising landscape is bees.

Bees just doing what they do, and Being and surviving.

It's Beautiful.

Lake Paika has recently been cleaned and refilled and I see many many black swans.

Just swimming, being graceful and gliding across the water.

Just being.

I sit and try over and over again to light the campfire beside the lake.

I poke, prod and continuously move the logs.

Upset, I then sit back and just let it be.

Flames I see

just being.

You see, all this is My Ideal Oneness—sitting on country on the land of my grandmother's birthplace. I travel here regularly when I need grounding and rest.

This is Love.

This is Home and this is all I need.

I gaze around, taking in the landscape, and I see peppercorn trees just being mystical and magical.

The saltbush is growing wildly and thriving. It just is.

Clouds roll slowly across the sky—just enough to hide the glare of the sun.

I watch the swallows dart around, welcoming me home to this space.

The old crow sings out.

The Old Man Eagle I finally and suddenly hear from afar. He's coming to greet me.

I feel love in this moment.

I feel the wisdom of the land harmonising with my footsteps.

I feel the emotion rise.

Why do we trick ourselves to search for beauty and magic and love in the big frantic rush of life?

This is my Love—when I am stillness, when I just BE, I am reminded I am Love.

I know that I have come through a deep, deep journey of lifelong healing. I had to hold on tight.

I was scared I wasn't worthy of love, or I couldn't absorb love from others.

I love my husband, children, and grandchildren greatly. That all seems easy, they are my heartbeat.

However, one day in my late forties, I realised I had stopped loving myself.

I was healing.
I moved through great trauma.
I gave service to others in my work and career.
But I still did not love myself or know how to. I thought there was a certain technique or prescription.

What is love anyway?
Who defines it for us?

What I do know is true though, is when I sit in the mallee bush on the riverbank or on Lake Paika I hear my breath—I feel love flow through me.
This is love in its purest form, I am sure.

When we just BE.
We are Love.
We become Love.

I have struggled all my life with feeling loved physically—I was orphaned as a toddler—and I somehow knew I was surrounded by this love bubble of my large extended family that raised me, but I never heard the words! It was just a knowing, I guess. I have been in very deep deep dark places, where I could not see, feel or hear love. Sometimes even today.

But I know society fucking tricks, scares and exploits us all!

We have to BE everything else, be better, be smarter, be prettier, be more spiritual, be good, be a good or better wife, mother and friend.

I think fuck that!

I am Love.
My Ancestors are Love.
My Culture is Love.
My wisdom and knowledge are Love.
My self-care is Love.

We all can be that.
Just like the Bees going about their day, doing their thing, just being.
The Black swans gracefully floating on the Lake.
The Trees are just standing their ground and blowing in the wind.
We just have to BE.

We have to reach deep deep inside and call out our name—I'm fucking home!

Here I am.

I am Love.

Sometimes we forget where home and our sacred space is ... it's within us.

Don't wait for someone to tell you, *You are good enough to be love and be loved.*

Tell your goddamn self.

Just be it.
It's not that complicated.
Take the pressure off, the pressure to perform, to be the best, to be

everything everyone else wants us to BE.

Just Stop.
Be still and Breathe, your Breath came from the Ancestors.
From Mother Earth.
With whom We Breathe in sync with every moment.
When others consume our energy, we fall out of sync.

I stood in the exact spot today where I had felt my grandmother's and ancestors' warm, gentle breath and kisses surrounding me at the Lake many years ago. It was a very magical, spiritual and healing moment in my life. I was reminded that I can just close my eyes and breathe and be back at that moment anytime. That's my medicine, being here is my medicine, being love is my medicine and to just BE is the Medicine for all.

I sometimes question, is my own medicine enough, is my healing enough.

I'm still alive, I'm breathing and in sync with Mother Earth at every moment.

Know what your BE is.
Then just do that.

It is really that simple.

# About the author

## Annabelle Sharman

Annabelle Sharman is a writer, healer, visionary and consultant. Founder of A Sharman HOPE Healing, Live in Oneness®, Spirit Cloth Creator and Yuma Yarns. Annabelle is a proud Mutti Mutti Woman living Self, Spirit and Mother Earth, who honours ancestral cultural heritage, knowledge, wisdom and a natural attuned connection to Earth medicine.

A passionate humanitarian with a Dreaming to heal Australia. Her deep personal and professional experiences, weaved together with ancestral knowledge, spirit and wisdom guides every aspect of her consultancy and healing work.

*"...sometimes we forget where home and our sacred space is ... it's within us ..."*

**liveinoneness.com.au**

# 2.

# The truth about quitting
## LAURA MAYA

It happened on a poorly lit street in Central America, back in March 2004. In a country with one of the highest homicide rates in the world, I was pulled by my ponytail from the back seat of a taxi and held up at gunpoint by six guys with machine guns.

It was the second time I'd been attacked since arriving in Honduras so I vaguely knew what to do: Stay calm, surrender my valuables and resist the urge to fight back. Only this time, when I thrust my handbag at one of the attackers, he snatched it, sneered and tossed it onto the street without checking inside. I remember looking down at my discarded bag lying in the gutter and back to his tattooed face in utter confusion. If they weren't after my money, what the hell *did* they want?

In the brief interlude after I realised this wasn't a robbery and before the universe intervened and orchestrated my escape, I felt what it was like to have my freedom taken away from me. To have no control over my own fate. To know that my heart's next beat was entirely dependent on a stranger with his finger on the trigger. And that experience is—I believe—why several years later I ended up becoming involved in the new abolition movement to end human trafficking and modern slavery. Because for the briefest and most terrifying moments of my life, I'd felt the fear and helplessness of being held captive. But unlike millions of others, I got away.

While we cowered on the street at the mercy of those men and their weapons, a police car suddenly screamed around the corner with its sirens blaring. Instantly, the men evaporated, scattering into cars and alleyways like cockroaches scurrying into the sewers. Gratefully, I'll never know what they wanted from me because I had the good fortune of being able to sprint down that dark, empty Honduran street towards freedom.

I got lucky, so years later I would make it my mission to be that screaming siren for someone else.

When I first learnt about the existence of human trafficking and slavery in modern times, I was stunned. Weren't we always taught that slavery was abolished in the 1800s and relegated to the history books? I had no idea that an estimated 40.3 million people were still enslaved today in situations of forced labour, sexual servitude and debt bondage, or that there are more slaves in the world now than at any other time in history. When I found this out, I was immediately triggered.

Dr Martin Luther King Jr famously said, '*No one* is free until we're *all* free,' and this truth set me on a journey of activism, which led me to anti-trafficking projects in Romania, the Netherlands, India and eventually Nepal. In Nepal, myself, my husband, David, and our family founded two grassroots non-profit organisations aimed at fighting slavery at the source. Instead of rescuing victims from the hands of traffickers, we wanted to find solutions for the problems that led them there in the first place. We approached human trafficking as a preventable disease. Early warning signs included poverty, poor education, unemployment, and gender and caste inequality. We hoped that if those symptoms were caught and treated early, we might find a cure.

We spent many months over many years living in a remote village of the Nepali Himalayas, trying to support the locals with their efforts to improve education and employment opportunities—so they could live and work in their own community, free from risk of exploitation, safe and surrounded by the people they love.

It's important to explain all of this so you understand just how personal and critical this work felt for me. I need you to know how this journey started so I can talk honestly about how it ended.

Because this is not a story of triumph or some fairytale about me saving the world. This is a story about how I failed and what happens when we quit.

Buddha himself, who was born in Nepal, said everything is temporary, and he was right. *Life* is temporary and so is everything that happens between the bookends of birth and death. Yet too often we expect the events in between to last forever, as if life is an endurance test. If you've ever tried and failed to achieve a goal, you'll know that no matter how challenging it becomes, quitting often doesn't feel like an option. We tell ourselves, *I made a promise … People are counting on me … But I'm so close … I've already invested so much time and money … What would people say?* Social media is awash with so-called inspirational quotes telling us *Winners never quit and quitters never win.*

But is that true?

***

Now I don't mean to brag, but when it comes to quitting things, I am *quite* the master ... I'm what some people call a multipotentialite—a hyper-curious person who feels called to explore many different careers, cultures, hobbies and interests instead of finding my 'one true calling' or somewhere to 'settle down'. My whole life I've struggled to finish the things I start because I'm always distracted by the billions of things I don't know that I don't know yet. Every day my mind generates so many ideas for dreams I could chase, businesses I could start, places I could live and skills I could learn that I'd need thousands of lifetimes to pursue them all.

This little personality 'quirk' is why I once went from working as a tax auditor in Amsterdam to being a nanny in Spain, then a barbecue chef in the Italian Alps. After that, I worked as a bar manager on a Scottish cruise ship before heading to Honduras to be a news journalist ... all within the space of two years. It's why I've invested a not-insignificant amount of time and money to become a qualified Zumba instructor, travel agent, sailor, kinesiologist, and massage therapist, yet I do precisely *none* of those things for a living now.

I churn through hobbies faster than I do toothbrushes. There was the ukulele phase ... the rollerskating phase ... the family-tree research phase ... and the 'how about I learn to ride a bike and cycle across an entire country' phase. And every time it's the same story. I start every new project like a kid tearing open a Christmas present, squealing, *It's just what I've always wanted, I will love it FOREVER!* But soon that new toy becomes old and starts collecting dust on the shelf while I skip off to play with something else.

I once flew all the way to Santorini to spend the winter months on a dormant volcano going to Greek school—despite having no Greek friends yet or any use for the language at all. Then once I'd learnt the alphabet and how to order a carafe of wine, that felt like enough ... so

I quit. Right now, I'm learning kung fu—an interest inspired mostly by my experience in Honduras but also because I'm curious to see if a squishy middle-aged woman can undergo the same transformation as a wobbly, dumpling-eating, cartoon panda. By the time you're reading this, I may have abandoned the martial arts to take up basket weaving. Or become an astronaut.

I'm a master of the art of calling it quits, so it should have come as no surprise to me or the people around me when I started a charity in Nepal, only to close it down a few years later. I mean, that's just how I roll, right?

No.

Not always.

Not when it comes to the big stuff.

I keep a small amount of stubborn determination reserved for the most important dreams and people I love. Fighting human trafficking was not a fleeting interest or passing phase. It felt like a mountain I'd been put on Earth to move. This wasn't like tinkering with the violin or learning to speak Klingon. In Nepal, people were counting on me and livelihoods were at stake. I'd made a promise to help improve education and employment opportunities in a remote mountain village and this time, quitting wasn't an option.

***

The leader of the village was Dar Kumari, an elderly Himalayan farmer of the indigenous Tibeto-Burman Gurung people. The first day we met in 2009, she told me to call her *Aama. Mother.*

Aama invited David and me to live with her family in their humble mudbrick home so we could build a library and establish an English teaching program at the struggling village school. Foreigners were rare on the mountain so Aama didn't quite know what to make of us at first and the feeling was definitely mutual. Everything I'd read about Nepal before arriving indicated many women were disenfranchised and oppressed. Village girls often had their marriages arranged in their teens and thousands were trafficked into unpaid labour and sexual servitude every year. In some parts of Nepal, girls were still born into slavery and women were banished to outdoor huts when they were menstruating, even though both practices were illegal. So I guess I had expected Nepali women would be meek, voiceless and disempowered. But that's not how I would describe my Nepali mother …

Aama is a blazing ball of sunshine who radiates enough light alone to illuminate all the women in her village. She's on the Mother's Committee, the Village Development Committee, the Health Post Committee and even the School Committee, despite never having learnt to read or write herself. Born into poverty, Aama married as a teenager and, against all odds, became one of the most prominent and respected decision makers in her husband's village. Now seventy, she climbs up and down her terraced fields with the confidence of a sure-footed mountain goat, often carrying the equivalent of her body weight in firewood, crops and manure in handwoven baskets on her back.

Aama seems fearless. I once watched her climb up a rickety wooden ladder to a traditional log beehive and—without any protective clothing—smoke the bees out with a flaming stick of fire. They charged at her and stung her face but she was grinning the whole time, delighted as she extracted a fistful of honeycomb and dropped it into a metal bowl with a satisfying clammer. Then she jumped to the ground and bounded off into the fields to harvest the potatoes for dinner, refusing all offers of help even though her face was engorged with bee venom and her eyes were swollen shut.

I was in awe of this woman. In the face of endless adversity, she showed a strength, stoicism and perseverance I rarely saw in myself. Yet for some reason she had put her faith in us to help her community and I was terrified of letting her down.

In the beginning, we worked at a village level, collaborating with her community to build a school library, a solar-powered computer lab and some home-based family microbusinesses. Our months in the Himalayas turned into years and we slowly expanded our work, providing educational scholarships to human trafficking survivors and at-risk communities in other parts of Nepal. After a few wrong turns at the start, we learnt it was crucial to take a community-led approach so the people who stood to benefit from our help were always in the driver's seat, calling the shots and in full control of their own destinies. We wanted to strike the right balance between offering enough support to empower people, but not so much that we impinged on their autonomy and progress couldn't be sustained without us.

It was a lofty goal.

We could build a library and fill it with books, but many of the students were malnourished and couldn't concentrate enough to read them. We could provide one hot meal at the school every day to alleviate their hunger, but it wasn't enough to ease the daily financial burdens faced by subsistence farming families who generate no income. We could train an entire community in the art of bee breeding so they could sell honey for profit, but they wouldn't earn as much money at home as their daughter could working as a housemaid in India.

We could run awareness campaigns to help people understand that seeking employment abroad puts them in danger of being trafficked, but we couldn't convince anyone that the risk of a future unknown was worse than the certainty of the poverty that gripped them now.

The first time a girl I loved went missing, I felt personally responsible. I berated myself for not doing enough to help. I barely slept for months after she disappeared, replaying every conversation I'd had with her on a loop in my head. I started questioning if I was the right person to be doing this work at all and it became increasingly harder to stand up in front of the crowds who gathered at our fundraisers and ask them to donate to projects that were falling short.

Yet still we persevered, because people were counting on us. Aama was counting on us. We'd started something and we weren't finished. I wanted to fight human trafficking like Aama carries a basket of buffalo poo up a Himalayan mountain—with strength, grit and a never-say-die determination. No matter how hard it got, no matter what life threw at her, Aama didn't quit, so how could I? So I put my game face on and tried to make it look like I was striding confidently forward, while inside I was staggering knee deep into the mud.

\*\*\*

I remember the day the end began.

I was sitting in a bustling cafe, tasked with the excruciating job of telling a mother that her young daughter had likely been trafficked to Kathmandu, was now untraceable and may never find her family again. Sitting there, I got the sensation that all the love I could pour into this cause was held in a porcelain vessel in my heart. It contained a finite amount of liquid and with every act of service, I released one tiny drop. But while trying to hold space for this heartbroken woman, I felt the porcelain crack. Soon the liquid was gushing out uncontrollably until there was nothing left inside me but a shattered, empty shell.

Numb, I spent the next three years stumbling forward, ashamed that I was too weak to continue but also too scared to quit. I clung on until I completely burnt out ... *then* we decided to close one of our charities and slowly wind down the other. The programs that were working well no longer needed our assistance and the ones that had failed would never be sustainable without us. Finally, following many long conversations, and with the support of our partner organisations, Aama and the community, we made the agonising decision to quit. After years of volunteering and struggling to make ends meet, it was time to turn the page.

We spent the next chapter of our lives working on a tiny island in the South Pacific Kingdom of Tonga. With plenty of time to stare out at the ocean horizon and reflect on our experience in Nepal, I came to accept an uncomfortable truth.

I'm a quitter.

I quit things. All. The. Time.

Not many people aspire to be a 'quitter', which the Oxford English Dictionary defines as someone who gives up easily or does not have the courage or determination to finish a task. Quitting is seen as a sign of weakness in our culture, where it's drummed into us that we'll be rewarded for our perseverance, so we should #NeverGiveUp.

But as I've slowly unpacked the outcomes of my seemingly endless string of failures, I've come to realise that's not always true. Sometimes quitting is an act of strength, like: *I quit drinking and turned my life around.*

Quitting can be an act of empowerment, as in, *I quit my secure, well-paid job to chase my dream and open my own cafe.*

Quitting can also be an act of love—*I gave it everything I had in me and I wanted it more than anything in the world ... but when it came at the expense of my health, I quit.*

Author and entrepreneur Seth Godin argues that winners are the people who 'quit fast, quit often, and quit without guilt'. They know whether they should keep pushing forward when things get hard, or if they've reached a dead end and there's nowhere to go. At that point, it can take just as much courage and determination to walk away, and a winner knows that sometimes quitting is the only way forward.

Today, I still aim to finish everything I start. I chase down my dreams like they're the last bus home ... but I never dismiss the urge to quit when she taps on my shoulder. Maybe she's whispering, *There's another way*, or *It's time to make room for something else.*

The truth is, not everything we take on in life needs to be an ultramarathon. Sometimes it's a sprint. Or a relay, where you go hard and then pass the baton to someone else on your team.

When I was drowning in shame as we wound up our work in Nepal, I wish I'd known it was ok to run a short race, that it was reasonable to take time out for an injury; because it's just as hard to run a race on a broken leg as it is to run a charity with a broken heart. I wish I'd known it was ok to slip out of my spandex, put on a comfy tracksuit and go sit in the grandstand with a bucket of fries and cheer on the next round of athletes.

Because that's where I'm most comfortable these days—on the sidelines with my pompoms, screaming words of encouragement to the people still in the arena. I quit and the world didn't end, but unfortunately neither did modern slavery. So now I'm the person I used to rely on—the donor who throws money at fundraising campaigns and signs petitions. I rock up to the homes of friends who are giving a lot to others and cook them dinner or do a load of laundry. We even took Aama on her first-ever holiday to give her a well-earned break after decades of tireless, backbreaking work. Eventually we realised the best way to help might not be to run the race ourselves, but to focus on filling up Aama's cup so *she* can keep pouring it out for the people in her community.

Yes, it's a wonderful feeling to finish something you start and realise a dream you've worked hard to achieve. But it can also be incredibly liberating to stand in your truth and say, *I've reached my personal end point. It's time to move on.* I want to live in a world where people feel safe to change direction rather than committing themselves to a lifetime of misery because they thought they were supposed to 'never give up'.

So in case you need to hear this and no one has ever told you, YES, it's ok to quit sometimes. Yes, you can still be strong, determined and resilient *and* not finish that thing you started. Even if you're emotionally attached to the outcome. Even when you've already invested tens of thousands of dollars and several years of your life. And yes, even when you're terrified of letting someone down. Quitting may come after triumph, enlightenment or failure, but it always creates a space in your life, some magical wiggle room where you have the freedom to grow into the person you don't even know you're still meant to become.

# About the author

## Laura Maya

Laura Maya is a writer, coach and culturally curious "digital nomad" who has spent over 20 years wandering slowly through almost 60 countries. She is the author of Tell Them My Name (2021, the kind press) and curator of the self-coaching program GPS for the Soul. Laura prides herself on living simply, chasing impossible dreams and creating a life that supports and enhances the freedom of others. She currently lives on the road in Australia, moving around the country with her husband in a converted school bus named Maurice.

www.lauramaya.com
@lauramayawrites

# 3.

# When Saturn hadn't returned

## NATASHA PICCOLO

We all have a child.

We are all parents.

Whether you like it or not, you have been entrusted with this responsibility, simply because you are alive. Parenting is a universal truth, it's just that some of us are not privy to it, accepting this responsibility only when we have a physical child in our arms.

This child that you have been gifted simply wants love. This child wants affection. They want to be told that they are wonderful in all their messy glory. They need to hear that their fantasies matter, that their fear is real. So real in fact, that they need to be embraced to get through the night.

This child is constantly waiting for someone to turn on the light. They can't find the switch to turn on their night lamp. The child needs a level of attention to merely *survive*.

It's non-negotiable, this level of attention.

Your child lives within this current version of yourself. It is better known as your *inner* child. This beautiful, whimsical kid is in a constant game of hide-and-seek. At times, they find their hidey-hole and fall asleep there, midgame. They don't want to be found. Being found means they've lost the game.

The child wants to be swallowed up and kept safe in this mad world, swaddled in their beloved blanket that smells of Mother and is tattered at the edges. Each thread evidence of a love so strong it cannot be contained and so the warm material has begun to fray ...

It's safe enough there, in the hidey-hole. Knees pulled up to the chest, self-soothing and introspective, the child creates their own external womb space. And in that moment, she is the child and the mother.

And yet, the child wants to be seen. Not found, but seen. The 'finding' must be left for the child to do, in their own time, at the crux of adulthood.

You are the child.

You are the parent.

You are responsible for the raising of your soul. That is your birthright.

That's all this child ever wanted.

To be seen.

***

The Saturn return, for those not yet familiar, is an astrological concept that surrounds the notion of one's fate. This slice of fate, however, is not about the beautiful destiny that we are all conditioned to think we are entitled to, but more about the wrath of hardships: the *real* life lessons that have been hand-picked for us to have to deal with in this lifetime.

I couldn't get enough of this idea when I was first introduced to it at twenty-seven years old. I heard the term when I was fumbling through the overwhelm of podcast content on my streaming service of choice.

Intrigued? Absolutely! I was, after all, the age that Saturn supposedly dishes out those hard lessons to you.

So, what is it exactly? Astrologers say that 'your Saturn' refers to the major life lesson that you will encounter before the age of thirty. Fail to learn *that thing* that Saturn has prepared for you, and you get gifted another thirty-year cycle, so your next return would appear around your fifty-eighth birthday—another solid chunk of time to learn *the same* lesson. Fall short of the lesson yet again? Well, you get *another* beautiful gift wrapped in Saturn's rings around your ninetieth birthday.

This is not a piece about my first Saturn return.

This is an absolute, cathartic breakdown of the lesson I learnt before I hit my big Saturn. The parts of my teens and twenties that I simply could not hide from, despite the constant game of hide-and-seek that I had participated in, so readily, my whole life up until the point of my Saturn.

And the best part of this story is, I didn't even know I was playing until I flipped the lesson on its head and birthed a child of my own in potentially the most controversial year of them all—2020.

**Spring 2006**

My head hurt, again.

I was tired from overthinking. From only getting two hours of sleep and having to fake a smile as I got my sorry ass ready for school. I was the A-grade student, the social justice leader, *the one everybody could turn to*—adults and peers alike. I never stepped a toe out of line as a teen. I was the model kid.

Teacher's pet, a parent's dream.

This was all external. It was very real too.

But so was my internal world. This was a world of relentless thoughts, courtesy of a mind way too wise beyond its years. My mind belonged to a teenager who had absolutely no skills to handle it. My mind was also in the hands of two very loving parents who had no idea how to nurture it.

This was the mind of a teen girl with severe depression and anxiety who thought her battle with that was normal and one-hundred per cent helpless.

Completely helpless.

I required sleeping tablets to get through my final school exams— and I thought this was normal.

Riddled with Catholic school girl guilt, I would pray obsessively, rotating prayer positions in an attempt to self-soothe and in the hope of falling asleep at night. If I stuffed up a word or had a thought less than saintly, I would have to start the prayer cycle again—and I thought this was normal.

I would often lie awake, crying myself to sleep about a world too monstrous for me to truly understand, having never left the hub of my small community. When I couldn't sleep, I'd wake my sister and cry on her shoulder, looking for a parent in someone two years my junior.

I knew *that* was not normal.

My condition was not a predictable one. It was not 'textbook'. I was not from a broken home and had never really suffered from any trauma. The fact that I didn't tick the clinical boxes was even more isolating when I came to understand my diagnosis a good five years later, as a very uncertain twenty-something woman.

I was diagnosed with obsessive compulsive disorder—a very specific form of anxiety that leaves you feeling extremely untrusting and obsessed with the meaning of existence, on a daily basis. My reality felt catastrophic. That was the work of the mental illness chiselling away in my mind—carving a warped sense of unsafety. Later after years of psychological work, I learnt that this uninvited *friend* of mine had been with me forever. It was the part of me that feared *normal*.

There was a 'bigness' to life that my inner child just could not comprehend, although she desperately wanted to. She longed to understand and experience the *normal* that she feared. To be like the other kids, who just seemed to play without the burden of the world's terrorism concerns or the pain of witnessing someone's loneliness and feeling a guttural sense of empathy.

Dying to help her cause and herself, the child that I had unknowingly inherited started to peek out from inside her hidey-hole. At a ripe twenty years old, this child had grown into a woman who was very much over winning the constant game of hide-and-seek that she had been playing with herself.

She had, after all, become accustomed to winning by not being found—she was really good at participating in that way. But she was bored of her hiding spot. Of always winning and masking her truth.

She wanted out.

She was forced to look at it all—and by it all, I mean her entire life to date and what it had meant when her friend hit a tree and very unexpectedly died just before New Year's Eve in 2011.

Depression, anxiety, panic attacks—they all met grief that year. But Grief was extremely gentle, it was kind. It offered *perspective*. Reason for the cause of sadness. Validation for shameful bouts of emptiness. The other key players of the child's mind, especially self-sabotage, had never offered that before. The only thing that healed the systemically ingrained mental illness for this child was intuition.

The following of the nudges. The nudges gracefully pushed by the hand of grief.

This warranted sadness was safe, liberating even. It opened up a direct channel to Spirit/Source/God. The child began to communicate with her intuition—and spoke directly to her fear. It could no longer win because the darkness of death had reared its ugly head to show her that this game called Life is about trying to achieve balance.

The quest for balance is ultimately safe. It is *measurable*.

Light, shade.

Yin, yang.

Dark, light.

Day, night.

She learnt, hard and fast, that you need fear, sickness, grief, illness in order to appreciate the sun.

The universal experience of love, the rays on your face.

There was a new-found gratitude for the *wholeness* of life.

Finally, permission to *breathe*.

I woke up to Self in 2013.

I was sitting in lotus pose, the first time my body had felt the posture of my meditation seat. I was at a one-day yoga retreat. I was a yogic virgin—my first time hurt. It felt uncomfortable. I didn't know whether I should have asked to leave. Had I consented to this level of vulnerability?

All I can really recall from that day was that the concept of time was completely warped when I was in the throes of my first journey into deep meditation. My meditation teacher was kind. It was the first time I felt emotionally safe to release without shame or guilt.

There, amongst the circle of women, all experiencing some sort of heartbreak or burden, I found and collected my tears. I wasn't even aware that I was crying at the time, until my teacher gently placed a tissue on my cushion. Then, I was immediately pulled into my physical reality.

My shirt—damp.

My hair—wet.

My mind—fuzzy.

My confusion—heightened.

My curiosity, at large.

'You've opened the channel. Welcome. There is no turning back now,' she whispered in my ear while massaging my temples. The touch of her hands on my head was unnerving. It invited electricity, a vibration that I had never felt in my material body.

I was puzzled. What channel? What had I opened? Where had I *landed*? How do I exist past this point?

Before I could spend time in the mind-fuckery that was my first 'post-meditation high', I was yanked back into hypnotic brain waves by the sound of the teacher's voice. She invited us into a forest. We were instructed to follow the path past the streaming creek, up the bubbling brook, to smell the musty mould on the rock, embedded in clusters of moss. That's where we were asked to lay our head.

Flowers and foliage were also there, bright, bold and evergreen.

Then, when we were ready, we were invited to turn around and meet the person who was always there.

Behind a boulder larger than her, a child.

The child.

*My* child.

Me, at six years old.

She was compassionate without consciously knowing it. She wore a paint shirt and no shoes. Her hair was neat and her bangs—cut straight across her forehead—were the feature of her face. Her eyes smiled harder than her mouth. Big, brown, bold.

In that moment, she knew it all, and she knew she did.

She twirled, she pranced around the rock bed, knowing that she owned the natural space surrounding her, just as much as the trees and the birds did. She created a bubble that could not be touched, especially not by the misshapen adult that stood there, observing her.

In that moment, I recognised more about that little girl than I did the version of myself that had entered the meditation. This is what living *unconditionally* looked like.

This is what it felt like to live in a boundless mental state. There were no chains in the forest. There were no loud voices belonging to everyone else except her. There in the forest clearing, the silence killed the confusion. It undid all the useless work of the past twenty years.

She caught my eye and walked over, shyly.

*Dance with me.*

I could not pick her up, she didn't need to be held.

Instead, she chose to hold my hand.

At first, an awkward spin from me, trying not to take the lead in a space I truly did not understand yet. And then suddenly, the urge to leap. Then to land, then to shake.

Full-body shaking.

Full-body release.

Full-body expulsion of all the pain, the confusion and the uncertainty that fatigued my body.

I let go of being the over-performer in a life I did not yet understand how to harness.

We stared at each other. She was now observing me.

There was certainty in her expression. It was anything but vacant.

*Wake up, Tash.*

She had an adult timbre to her voice that resonated so deeply, it was jarring.

The voice again.

'Wake up, Tash.'

I wasn't sure who was speaking but I knew that the wisdom in the melodic intonation was far more sagacious than I could draw upon. Her face blended with my teacher's. My meditation seat was still. The only thing I was attuned to was the undeniable experience of *prana*—life force—vibrating up and down my spine.

The vibration felt *whole*.

For the first time in my life, I was aware of my breath.

Slow, bottomless, oceanic.

I finally understood the medicine in *taking a deep breath*. My mind's eye displayed a cinematic explosion of colour behind my eyelids. There was only love.

I was in the thick of the feeling only felt seconds before giving birth.

At that exact moment, I had become a parent.

A little girl.

My heart made room to hold that little girl in a way she had never been held before. I made a promise to her. She would never be unheard again.

This child, my inner child, was finally *seen*.

All her needs lay before me, unmet but intact. Ready to actualised.

This realisation was my awakening to Spirit. Saturn had not yet returned and yet this lesson, the need to consciously re-parent Self, was the pivot point for me that underpinned the rest of my twenties. I could not go back.

I vowed, when Father Saturn with rings of discipline chose to wrap his chokehold around my throat, I would never silence that little girl again. This I knew was true.

As my teacher had said, the channel was *opened*.

From that day onwards, I actively chose to live my life by observing the stream of consciousness that ran through my untamed mind.

Even in my dream state, my subconscious knew it had work to do to expel years of unprocessed content. Voices that did not belong to me. Faces left unnoticed. Memories discoloured.

Sepia …

Banished.

And the hiding spots, finally exposed.

The little girl forced a level of vulnerability that I had no choice but to embrace.

Just pure love.


**December 2020**

7:51 am on the third day of the festive season, I had my own festivity to show up for.

I was naked.

Dressed down to show up.

I had become a parent. Reborn. *Again*.

Nine years later.

My boy was absolutely perfect.

Saturn had made good innings; I was two months shy of his return when I became *Mother*. If the Spirit girl had made me a parent, my son had made me Mother.

The inner child of mine that resided lovingly in my heart shaped hidey-hole moved over that day. She made room, fluffed the pillows for her soul mate.

Not quite a big sister, but a guiding force.

She knew she would have a starring role to play in ensuring that this little soul would always know how to dance. She would show him how to express himself, how to keep his voice clear. How to paint, draw, skip and laugh.

She would one day expose the world's truths and help him find his stance on it all, all while recognising that he, a boy, a man in the twenty-first century, is ultimately *safe*.

The little girl would show him that all emotions are equal, purposeful and there to be felt. That you also have control over when they should be released. That you can decide which of them should serve you in any given moment.

She would show him that hide-and-seek is a game that shouldn't be played past the age of seven, the age we enter into conscious thought.

Of moral judgement.

Of rights and wrongs—bipolarities.

Most of all, as I locked eyes with my blue-eyed angel, I promised that being a Mother would never mean losing the voice of my inner child. My inner child would walk side by side with my son and teach him how to play with this life. A friendship, an eternal union that offered equal parts guidance and surrender.

The lesson Saturn didn't teach was this: The many roles we perform and will continue to star in will shapeshift. It's inevitable.

All versions of self, all roles, are equally valid.

Parenting may seem like an additional role, but it's simply an extension of you. The version of you that inherently knows blind faith, unwavering trust and unconditional love.

There is one variable that sets us apart as adults.

Those who choose to consciously unsubscribe from the never-ending game of hide-and-seek and those who aren't aware they are still playing, waiting for a parent to invite them out of the hidey-hole.

Find that child.

Embrace that child.

Validate their voice.

Invite them to come out and truly *play*.

# About the author

## Natasha Piccolo

Natasha Piccolo is a mama and small business owner. She is always up for a good chat as her main work roles include clinical Speech Pathology and life coaching. Her business, Resonate Holistic assists clients to facilitate healthy communication across the life span. Natasha also runs a gelato cart events business, Pina Piccolina, with her husband (the sweetest 'side hustle' out!) Natasha describes her life as full, fun and fulfilling.

Natasha is the author of The Balance Theory (2022, the kind press).

In her personal and professional life, it is the magic in people's stories that inspire her most. Natasha writes from a place of heart open honesty. Natasha hopes that her words motivate others to live a life that is consciously aligned. When she isn't singing her son nursery rhymes or is out of office, Natasha loves nothing more than a long brunch date, a juicy yoga sesh, a delicious tea and a great book.

**Instagram handle: Natasha Piccolo (author) @tashspeaks**
**Instagram handle: Resonate Holistic @resonate_holistic**
**www.resonateholistic.com.au**

# 4.

# The art of casual racism
## MEAGHAN KATRAK HARRIS

**The Mildura Show, early 1990s**

Mildura on the Murray River. The Heart of Sunraysia in North West Victoria. An artificial 'oasis' in the harsh Mallee landscape, rendered unnaturally green and fertile thanks to the Canadian Chaffey Brothers and the irrigation system they built in the late 1800s. Mildura would go on to be known as Australia's food bowl.

The politics of water and the looming disaster ahead for the Murray River hadn't yet reached you in the early 1990s. Mildura was considered a well-laid-out, attractive regional 'city'. Wide, green nature strips and tree-lined avenues. Apparently Australian gardening icon Kevin Heinz had visited sometime in the seventies or eighties, and was asked what would grow well here. 'Bottlebrush,' it is said he replied, offhandedly. He was taken at his word and street after street was now a frenzy of *Callistemon*, evergreen native shrubs whose red flower spikes form the exact shape of a bottlebrush.

Held annually, the Mildura Show is your typical country show. Noise and crowds, sideshows and rides that look glitzy and exciting at night and a bit tired and sad during the day, if you look too closely. Thrilling nonetheless for country kids and still considered a local highlight.

This particular year you and your partner had loaded the three kids into the beige Holden Commodore and driven ninety kilometres from your hometown of Robinvale to attend the show, along with at least half the community. You were a young mum, young enough that over thirty-five years later you understand that your daughter's birth created somewhat of a stir in sectors in your small hometown. That and your partner's Aboriginality.

You can remember when you got it, the Commodore. Your newest car yet. Current Shape, a real shift within the eighties and nineties when cars suddenly were smaller, boxier and looked more modern. It was a Big Deal to you and your partner, purchased during the days when you made an appointment with the local bank manager, and he looked at your job, looked at you, and decided if you were in stable employment and of good enough character to be given a loan to buy a car. Apparently, you both were. And your dad guaranteed it, so there was that too.

You remember when your partner walked in to pay for petrol not long after buying the Commodore (second hand, by the way), and a local asked him, 'Whose car?'

'Mine,' said your partner.

'Jeez,' said the local, 'Youse are getting better cars than us now.' *Youse* of course meaning Aboriginal people, *us* being him, the white man who, somehow by his way of thinking, should have had a better car by virtue of his whiteness. You remember you and your partner shaking your heads at the local's ignorance.

Robinvale (population 1600) was a young town, even by the metrics of the colonisers, the invaders. Less than a century old. A soldier settlement. Parcels of land called 'blocks' had been carved up and distributed to returned soldiers after the Second World War by the Government to grow grapes and citrus. The surrounding roads were later named after the battlegrounds these soldiers had returned from: Damascus Road, Crete Road, Malaya Road. A neat little town proud of its soldier settlement beginnings.

In the fiftieth-anniversary book *Robinvale … the first fifty years*, published in the 1970s, the town's historians document their prideful pioneer story.

In this story, Aboriginal people were not present in Robinvale prior to the township's establishment. The historians' version conveniently tells us Aboriginal people arrived in the area around the same time as the white settlers. Millenia of Aboriginal history would dispute that, and tell us that Aboriginal people always lived along the River. However, the historical committee felt confident enough to republish that same spiel thirty years later in the 2000s, for the eightieth anniversary—somewhat depleted and less excited celebrations. There aren't many original soldier settlers left now, or original family blocks. Aboriginal People are still here.

But on this day, the decision was what to do first at the Mildura Show. You and your partner decided to take the kids to the farm displays. They were probably more interested in the rides and showbags, but you two young parents did The Right Thing and headed to the agricultural show.

You were pushing the pram with the littlest baby boy, his primary-school-aged sister holding on, and the two-year-old being carried by their dad. You walked into the shed and started the procession around to look at the livestock. Sheep, definitely. Cows? Probably, you can't remember now.

It certainly smelled like a farm. All hay, dust, manure, the sharp stench that catches your nostrils. You grew up a 'townie' but were enough of a country girl that the farm display held no novelty for you.

An older farmer, very much looking the part in his beaten Akubra hat, was sitting in front of the sheep pens. (Now, in your mind's eye he was sitting on a hay bale, but that would be too clichéd. It was probably an aluminium fold-up chair.) You approached; kids interested, excited, your open-faced, open-hearted daughter smiling, your partner ready for a yarn (he loved a yarn, and people loved yarning with him). The farmer spoke loudly, to no one in particular, yet particularly to you. You were the only ones there.

'Have you heard about MABO?' he boomed, then quickly answered his own question. 'It stands for "Money Available; Blacks Only".' It hung in the air, this statement. Heavy, hovering. For a second you weren't sure where it would land.

The Mabo Case had been big in the news—Eddie Mabo's decade-long struggle for the Meriam People of the Murray Islands in the Torres Strait to be recognised as Traditional Owners of their Lands. This significant case challenged the existing Australian legal system's assumption of terra nullius, or empty land, and was being followed and celebrated keenly in the Aboriginal community while unearthing a barely concealed racist vein in the white.

You and your partner looked at each other. You weren't shocked, nor frightened, more … *Here we go* …

'Let's go,' one of you said. (You can't remember which.) You kept walking. Not today. That day the statement was stepped over, kicked to the side and given no space.

'We just wanted to show the kids the animals,' you said to the farmer as you passed, hoping to shame him. He wouldn't return your gaze. You headed back to Side Show Alley. The Black Man, the White Woman and their Three Brown Kids.

Something may have been muttered between you about what exactly he could do, that farmer, with his poxy sheep.

## Robinvale 1990s

You were sitting in the car in front of Fishers, the local supermarket. It must have been Christmas. You know this because your older brother was in the passenger seat next to you and it was a stinking hot day. He was home from Melbourne to visit, as he always did.

You two are very close even though he left for boarding school when you were eight or nine. At the time your auntie had said to your mum and dad that they were 'educating him above his station'. It doesn't seem to have done him any harm.

He was your link to the Bigger World, in many ways. He bought you books, CDs and cool T-shirts. He'd studied law and history and worked for Native Title. An intellectual who can scull a beer, kick a footy and throw a punch, if need be. He is the Rock Star of your family.

There was a tap on the window and standing there was a White Lady. Pastel blouse? Tick. Popped collar? Tick. Pearl studs? Tick. Puffed up with her own sense of entitlement? Tick, tick, tick.

She was tapping on the glass and you wound the window down. 'Are you the Harris girl?' she asked. 'The one married to an Aborigine?' Did she notice the sharp intake of breath from you and your brother? You doubted it.

'Yes,' you said. 'My name is Meaghan.' Even in your shock, you tried to humanise this exchange.

'I want to talk to you,' she said. 'I'm so worried about my daughter.'

You knew who she was, this woman. You knew who her daughter was. You knew where this was going. Her daughter was going out with an Aboriginal boy. Obviously creating a Stir in her family.

'My daughter is going out with …' she began.

'I know,' you responded, cutting her off. 'He's a nice boy.' She looked at you imploringly, obviously wanting more from you. You didn't know what.

'His family are good people,' you said. 'Very well respected.'

'But,' she lamented, 'he hasn't even got a car.'

The rest of this awkward exchange is a bit of a blur. You remember trying to convey your thoughts about good character being more important maybe? About their youth, there being time for establishing a job, a life, stuff? Your brother was aghast, bristling in the seat next to you.

The White Lady departed, with a pained expression that told you whatever she had wanted from you remained unfulfilled. What *had* she wanted from you? Not, it seems, reassurance of the character of the boy, or his family. You and your brother looked at each other. *You couldn't make this shit up*, you thought.

Thirty-odd years later, you think about the boy in question. He'd be a middle-aged man now. You look up his profile on Facebook. He looks good, standing next to his shiny car.

**Mildura mid 2000s**

Life went on with the big dramatic changes that crashed through your world and at times seemed to cause irreparable damage, but this now just felt like the ebb and flow of life. Marriages had come and gone, and come. You lived in Mildura now, right in Bottlebrush Central. Family had extended and blended, as they do, in multiple directions. New jobs, new home, new chapters.

You had two degrees in social work and were working at the

largest local service provider, managing family services programs.

You were walking in the sunshine one day, toward the local park, enjoying your new neighbourhood. An older man was approaching, obviously walking his dog, who was unrestrained and bounding slightly ahead. The dog (a Labrador cross maybe?) came towards you. You're a bit scared of dogs so extended a friendly greeting to the dog, while eyeing the owner, hoping he would catch up soon.

'Come on, Rosie,' the man called to his dog as he came closer, crossing the grass towards you. He stopped and looked at you. 'Rosie doesn't like Blackfellas. Do you, Rosie?' he said, addressing the dog as he put on the leash.

Your chest tightened. You paused and looked around. *Who is this man? Does he just greet everyone on the street that way?* You know he must have seen your family. Your big brown sons. The gang of brown and black boys who hang out at your home too.

The statement felt menacing. You didn't look at the man, but addressed the dog. 'Don't you, Rosie?' you asked. Your voice sounded falsely lighthearted in your ears. 'Well, we can't be friends then.' You turned and kept walking.

The whole exchange, only a few minutes in length, left you feeling winded.

### Robinvale 2010s

You were home to visit from Sydney, on break from your university lecturer job that you had secured soon after completing your PhD. Life in Sydney was different, but rich in its own way. Gathering at your parent's place in Robinvale; kids, grandkids, your folk's great-grandkids—it's always good to be home.

One of your sons had driven down from Mildura and was relaying to you how he was stopped by the police driving down the main street of Robinvale. Well, the only street really.

Licence and registration were checked and in order. 'Whose car?' he was asked by the policeman, referring to his new (second hand) Holden Commodore.

'Mine,' he replied.

'Where'd you get it?' asked the policeman.

'I bought it.'

'How?'

'With money. I've been working since I was seventeen.'

'Youse are getting better cars than us,' replied the policeman, who sent him on his way.

### Sydney 2021

It was your usual midweek dinner catch up with your daughter's family. Life was busier and fuller since they had made the move to the city too. Over a big, chaotic meal, you shared all the news. Your daughter Leshae had started a new job and was telling the story of a greeting from a colleague.

'Most importantly,' they had said to her before any other introductions were made, 'what do you like to be called—Aboriginal or Indigenous?'

'Leshae is fine,' she'd responded wryly.

### This I Know is True

These exchanges of so-called casual racism are so frequent and flippant that they speak volumes about the psyche of white Australia. People are seen, judged and categorised with breathtaking ease.

Back home you felt part of the Aboriginal community you lived in. Much more so than the white community, if you had to delineate between the two. Of course, they intersected, and the townsfolk would have many examples of how integrated the town was, in lots of ways. On the surface. On the football field.

Back home, back then, you were so confident in your place. The confidence born from love and acceptance within the Community. It felt clearer to you, your position, unquestioned, before community morphed into work and you realised that your white self might be Taking Up Too Much Space. That you might be Overconfident in your place. The kind of unquestioning confidence that can be born from (yet unrecognised) white privilege itself.

This would, over the years, play out with great complexity for you internally. There's an intricacy to the insider/outsider dance that is hard to get right. Too many steps forward or too many back? You still feel the pain of it, the weight of it, the joy of it.

You know now, we are all more than one story.

# About the author

# Meaghan Katrak Harris

Meaghan is the author of *Memories and Elephants: The Casual Art of Racism* (2022, the kind press). Meaghan is a social worker, academic, consultant and writer. She has a long and diverse social work practice background. This includes extensive experience and commitment to working alongside First Nations Peoples, families and communities. When not writing, Meaghan is currently lecturing and researching in social work at Sydney University and working in private practice across social work supervision, individual, group work and organisational change.

# 5.

# No matter what happens in life, you always have yourself

## JO KENDALL

The day I was told I had cancer was one of the most surreal days of my life.

My experience through cancer and dealing with the ups and downs of the many emotions, thoughts and fears that naturally were present—as well undergoing physical treatments—was deeply humbling and taught me the most I have ever learnt about myself. And if I were to distil all of this down to one profound key learning, it is undoubtedly that no matter what happens in life, you always have yourself.

My name is Jo Kendall, and this is a small part of my story.

While my story is one of moving through and overcoming cancer, this is only one story in a million that could apply to the things I am about to share with you. You may find this a strange thing for me to say, but cancer was the catalyst for me to become the most empowered version of myself yet, and for that I have nothing but gratitude.

You see, we all have challenges in life that can leave us feeling like we are on our own. No matter how much others are there to support us personally or professionally, at the end of the day, it is our own mind and thoughts that we need to harness to be our very own guide and source of light and comfort. It is our thinking, our mindset and our actions that are the difference that makes a difference. We need to be our own best ally and have our own back in every moment.

Through my journey with cancer, I learnt this in a way I never had before. And while cancer was my lesson, we all have our own version of this.

Now, I am not sure what you will make of this, but not long before I was diagnosed, I had set a goal and embarked on a one-hundred-day challenge of meditating daily. To say I am thankful to past Jo is an understatement, and I am sure that my inner wise woman had well and truly taken the steering wheel with this. This was a saving grace for me and one of the biggest things that helped me through the initial diagnosis and being told I had cancer and then undergoing multiple surgeries, all while the world shut down with COVID-19.

There were times I would meditate up to three times daily. I learnt how to interrupt intense spirals of fear and doubt and effectively bring myself back to a place where I felt calm and would focus on and visualise the best possible outcome. This practice enabled me to walk into hospital alone (as no one was able to be with me because of COVID) calmer and more centred over time, have my own back, and be my own source of comfort and love.

I attribute this to my surgery successes, of course not taking away from the incredible surgeons and nurses nor the love and support of my family, who were all instrumental and part of my recovery—*but* so was I. It was my ability to be my own source of calm, find steadiness and peace within, and do the inner work that allowed me to ask and honestly answer tough questions such as, *If this were happening for my highest good, what could that be? What is draining my lifeforce? What do I really want to do with my life?* and *What makes me feel most alive?* And through all of this I became very clear on what truly mattered, on how I wanted to live and that I unwaveringly felt and knew I had so much to live for. This resulted in my very last surgery being better than expected, with the best possible outcome, very minimal time in hospital, and a fantastic recovery. And I have since become healthier and healthier every day.

We each have within ourselves a truly great strength, and when we remove doubts, fears and beliefs that hold us back, we can move into the most sovereign of beings. No matter what situation life presents us, we can be the calm in the chaos. We have ourselves, in the big and small life moments. And of course, it is not just in my personal experience that I have seen this firsthand but also with the thousands of people I have worked with over the years in a counselling, coaching and leadership capacity.

My words here serve to give you an insight into the extent to which working within myself—applying meditation and a healthy and positive mindset—helped me move through one of the most challenging times of my life. My experience and new-found learnings lit something inside of me and I went on and studied meditation therapy as a postgrad and have now completed my Advanced Diploma. I am passionate about helping people realise that meditation does not have to be sitting still for thirty minutes thinking no thoughts. Instead, meditation is a way of *being*, and there are as many ways to meditate as there are people. To this end, I have developed a framework that allows people like you to create their very own personalised meditation practice, one that suits their lifestyle and evolves as they do.

Let us now walk through four key components that will empower you to always have yourself.

**You are your own best ally**

I get it; in times of hardship, it can be difficult to keep your mindset on top of things. When we are told bad news, or news that changes the course of our lives dramatically, telling ourselves that we are fine and that there are better days ahead can quite simply feel like we are lying to ourselves.

This is not about being in denial and pretending things aren't the way they are, but rather recognising that the mental tape we have playing is something we have immense power over. The way you perceive anything and everything in life will determine your thoughts, and your thoughts will determine your emotions. And the only person who has a real impact on how you perceive what is happening is, well, you! The beliefs you hold about yourself and your potential, especially in challenging times, can either support you in moving forward positively or hold you back from experiencing things the way you want to experience them. As such, they have a fitting name: limiting beliefs.

It is very common for people to throw around the statement *Believe in yourself*. But, have you ever questioned what it is that you actually do believe? This is the best place to start; by examining your beliefs with love and curiosity and leaving out the self-judgement, you can begin to identify where your thoughts are holding you back. And from here, you can take the steps needed to rewrite your beliefs and create your very own internal support system, where your beliefs align with what it is that you really want. This will enable you to create a clear path forward instead of remaining stuck or being pulled backwards because what you are saying you want differs to that which you actually believe to be true (we are not always conscious of our beliefs).

As you can imagine, limiting beliefs create all kinds of havoc and dissatisfaction and are the reason you're not moving in the direction you want to be. We need to get this part on track before any of the other tools will work effectively.

Doubt your doubts. This powerful little instruction was shared with me many years ago and is something I still do to this day. Your doubts are only one way of looking at and thinking about a situation or yourself. And by questioning fear-based thoughts and their validity, we start to see they are not rock solid at all and we open our minds to new thoughts and beliefs that are on par with our most desired outcome.

An example of a fear-based thought is, *I don't think I can do this.* Ask yourself whether this is completely true—unwaveringly so? The answer to this is no, it's not true. So, we then ask, *If I could do this, what would that look like? How would I do that? What is one small thing I could do?* And just like that, you have switched your mindset from can't to can and opened yourself up to possibility.

One of my favourite quotes is by Henry Ford: 'Whether you think you can, or you think you can't—you are right.'

Henry has this spot on. Our beliefs serve as a self-fulfilling prophecy; what you believe to be true about yourself and your perception of your life are what you will see and experience. So, with this in mind, wouldn't it be wise to consciously take control and harness the power of your thoughts and create and hold beliefs that see you living as the healthiest, happiest, most whole and complete version of yourself? The you that moves through challenges with grit and grace, the you that is clear, calm and confident and knows that as Dr John DeMartini says, everything in your life is on the way, not in the way.

Specifically, this all means one thing: be your own best ally!

You have control over what you think and believe, and whilst the circumstances you find yourself in may not be something you have any control over, you do get to choose how you respond. Your beliefs will either limit or empower you.

In my case, throughout my cancer journey every day, and in every moment, I choose to empower myself through my thoughts. And you can do this too.

**Your mindset is what makes you grow**

Having a positive mindset allows one to view challenges and struggles from a more optimistic perspective. This is called the 'growth mindset'—a term coined by Dr Carol S Dweck, who states that there are two mindsets that we humans primarily operate from, growth or fixed.

A fixed mindset, as the name suggests, keeps you stuck in your current situation, whereas a growth mindset allows you to grow and evolve and create and live your ideal life with the belief that you can and will reach it. Having such a mindset is key for self-development, but more importantly it is key when it comes to facing challenges where you feel that you have little to no control. Having a growth mindset here makes all the difference in the end.

A growth mindset is simply one that enables you to view things or situations in a positive and open manner. Positive thinking also enables you to address challenging situations with poise and courage, encouraging growth. Positive thinkers are less anxious and tense, less depressed, and have a better self-image than those with a fixed mindset skewed towards negative thinking.

Furthermore, a positive mindset leads to a more fulfilled and happier life. Why? Simple: when we are operating from a fixed mindset, we are completely closed to the myriad of possibilities, solutions, and growth options available. So life is only being partly lived, with a cap on personal fulfilment and possibility coupled with negative thought patterns, which results in an adverse feedback loop. Think about it this way: when you wake up on the wrong side of the bed, in a bad mood, does the bad mood usually stick around? Do you feel like every other thing that happens that day is a hundred times worse than it usually would be? And the next day, when you are in a better mood, do you realise that all the things you thought were terrible yesterday perhaps weren't so terrible after all? Yes, we've all been there. This is what it means to be in a negative feedback loop, and while we all have these days from time to time, we can choose for this not to be our whole life.

Studies have shown that a positive attitude in life benefits your mental, physical, emotional and spiritual wellbeing as it keeps you focused on the things that make you feel happy and bring you joy, which produces more feel-good chemicals in the brain and moves endorphins throughout your body. People with a growth mindset succeed more because they are open to possibilities and believe they can succeed. They see life's challenges as opportunities to learn and grow and become better, stronger and wiser than before—a more fulfilled and whole version of themselves.

Those with a positive mindset also experience lower stress levels and an overall sense of fulfilment. Positive thinking will allow you to be and feel more optimistic, and have the confidence to take aligned risks and go after your dreams, engage in creative activities and pursuits, and challenge conventional wisdom simply because you believe it's worth it! Because you're worth it!

Putting focus on the negatives will keep you from overcoming and moving through challenges, whereas positive thinking will allow you to turn those challenges into learning experiences, and become more apt and stronger because of it. We can foster positive thinking and a growth mindset by training our minds to focus on what we *can* do in any given situation—and, my friend, the very good news is, there is always something that you can do.

**Be kind to yourself**

Oh, such a simple and underrated idea. Be kind to yourself. You will never speak to anyone more than you speak to yourself in your head, so we want to make this a kind place to be.

First, it's about becoming aware—noticing the dialogue, both conscious and unconscious. It's not about judging yourself as good, bad, right or wrong, instead it is just being aware of the mental tape that's playing.

One of my favourite tools for bringing ourselves into the present moment is simply our breath—a deep inhale and a calm exhale, noticing the natural pauses at the end of each exhale. When you breathe out, there is likely to be a subtle pause just before you inhale. Notice this natural point of stillness. It is a tiny moment of calm and when you focus on it, your attention becomes present. It helps you let go of any thoughts about the past or future and allows you to be right here, right now.

And it is from this place, with a settled nervous system, that we can look at things objectively and choose to move forward with kindness and love.

I can tell you that this simple little practice is something I personally use daily and leant on firmly during my cancer journey. Our breath is a way for us to regulate our emotional self and interrupt any unhelpful thoughts and instead choose kind, supportive and beneficial beliefs. This can take time and practice but can change your life in ways you may not even be able to fathom yet.

When going through challenging times, be sure to show yourself compassion and kindness. It's so easy to love ourselves on our good days but we need that same love, kindness and compassion even more when we're feeling less than or scared and facing difficulties—being kind to ourselves during these times is one of the most powerful things we can do.

Something I have done and recommend to my counselling and coaching clients is to write a list of all the things you can do to show kindness to yourself. Whilst the answers vary, generally speaking, it is about identifying what we find grounding and nurturing and what gives us a sense of peace and calm within. Write those things down and make time for them, not just during hardship, but throughout your entire life.

Think about this: you are with yourself always, you are never not with yourself, so it stands to reason that being kind, caring and considerate to yourself in the same way you are to others is only ever going to be highly beneficial and vastly improve the quality of your one beautiful life.

**Make time for yourself!**
The final point I want to put forward in this chapter is the benefit that meditation can bring. Although at first this may evoke thoughts of needing to be very still or sit in a certain (uncomfortable) position and not think any thoughts, I assure you meditation is much more than these things.

Meditation is thousands of years old. It has been done by all kinds of individuals, from monks to celebrities to everyday people. It is both a spiritual practice used within Eastern religions and in the business, sporting and medical worlds for stress management and to assist in developing a healthy mindset and way to relax.

After studying postgrad meditation therapy, and having a dedicated practice myself, it is my experience and view that meditation is a way of *being*. And we each experience this in our own way; it may be breathwork or mindfulness or a mix of yoga and focusing on stretching the body, all of which are therapeutic. Meditation can be active and dynamic; it can be highly visual (a personal fave) or it can be quiet and still. It is what gives you a sense of peace and brings you back to *yourself* over and over and over again.

Almost all of us have meditated in one form or another, perhaps you were washing the dishes or waiting in line for your morning coffee or standing in the shower with the warm water running over your body and your mind wandered. This is meditation. Any time you catch yourself daydreaming and unaware of your surroundings, you have just been in a meditative state. And by bringing intention and clarity to this, you can create your own meditation and personalised peace practice that works with your rhythms and evolves as you do.

So, this is your invitation to relearn what you think meditation is and isn't and create your own unique practice and enjoy the many benefits that you will undoubtedly experience.

Ultimately, I want to circle back to those four key points before we close out our time together here in these pages.

First, be your own best ally. Life is uncertain and things can always happen unexpectedly. What you know is that you will always have yourself, so be the best and truest version of yourself and tap into the innate strength and wisdom you have within to truly have your own back in any and all of life's situations.

Second, your mindset is instrumental in you either not moving forward in life and staying stuck in a negative feedback loop *or* creating and living the life of your dreams, seeing possibility and opportunity in all of life and making the best of it with gratitude and love.

Third, be kind to yourself. Don't underestimate the power of being kind to your mind, body and spirit. Write out a list of ways you can do this every day for the rest of your beautiful life. And speak to yourself with kindness and love in the same way you would to those who matter most to you.

And finally, make time for yourself. Learn to meditate in a way that is supportive to you and your lifestyle, remembering this is a practice and tool that should not be stressful but seamless, and a way for you to feel grounded, clear and calm in any circumstances you find yourself in.

Thank you for being here and sharing in these words with me. I will leave you for now with the following: No matter what happens in life, there is one thing I know to be true, and it is the one thing I want most for you to know too: you *always* have yourself.

# About the author

# Jo Kendall

Counsellor, Coach + Meditation Therapist

With over 20 years' experience and having worked with thousands of people from all over the world, Jo specialises in helping you slow down and find your own rhythm and teaches how we can each access unwavering resilience within and be our own best ally throughout any life situation one finds themselves in. Jo does this through one-on-one sessions and online programs + services drawing on the latest teachings in psychology, meditation therapy and her own life experiences and personal story.

Offerings

Counselling and Coaching with me 1:1:

www.jokendall.com/1on1sessions

Find Your Own Mediation Rhythm Masterclass (FYOMR):

www.jokendall.com/fyomr

**www.jokendall.com**

**jo_kendall**

# 6.

# The little moments that can change everything

## MARITZA BARONE

Let's face it, we all have specific moments in our lives that change us. Life-defining experiences that happen, and then we are never the same.

For most of my life, I had always thought these experiences had to be significant life events, like the loss of a loved one, an illness, an accident, bankruptcy, divorce or other difficult situations ... but I later realised there are very small moments in our lives that can have the same impact and spark change. Especially if we are aware.

There was one morning I woke up and was doing the usual rush around, trying to get myself out the door for work. As a TV producer and presenter, I had a big filming day ahead and I needed to be out of the house early, ready to manage the shoot. I had been planning this day for weeks and was anxious and excited.

I was trying to get myself ready, wake and dress my kids, brush their knotty hair, pack lunches, make breakfast, and get my resistant daughter's damn socks on. The kids were playing up, and things we not going as planned time-wise. I was going to be late, and I despised being late.

Tension was rising and I just wanted to get out of the house and to work without all of the added pressure. 'Just for once,' I kept saying under my breath. I felt bitter and wondered why, for just this one day, things couldn't go smoothly. And so, I snapped. It all got too much. I stomped around the house, yelled at my poor children and husband, felt completely victimised, and slammed the front door in a huff and with no sweet goodbyes. Not the scene I had imagined when planning a family of my own.

I remember sitting in my car, devastated and so rattled by my behaviour, hoping that my kids we too young to remember how I had just acted.

I think back now, and it was such an accumulation of things that led me to that childlike tantrum, but I wasn't conscious enough at the time to see the cause.

I dusted myself off, put my car in drive and headed to the shoot. When I got there, I acted as though nothing had happened. I plastered a big smile across my face and proceeded to have my 'amazing' shoot day. But I wasn't aware that this day was going to change my life.

I was the producer on this shoot, which had us interviewing a single mum who had been through significant financial struggles. She had been completely broke, sleeping on her friend's couch with her young baby for months and trying her best to find a way to survive and create a life for herself and her son.

As she shared her experiences, I felt tears slowly roll down my face. I was hypnotised by her story and how she had overcome these testing times. She was in a wonderful place now, had built a thriving business from the ground up and finally got herself off her friend's couch and bought her own home.

I needed to know more. I needed to know how she could manage raising a child alone, building a successful business and being blissfully happy, and why I (with a home, partner and steady finances) couldn't even get to a workday without blowing up at my family. *I should be happy, shouldn't I?* I asked myself. Didn't I have everything I was always told I needed? I felt like a failure. A failure at work, a failure at home and a failure in my relationship, which had also not been going well for some time.

I pulled her aside after the shoot and told her that her story had moved me so deeply. I asked her how she did it, how she survived, what her secret was to being happy and how she did it all on her own. She looked at me with a knowing smile and walked me over to her bookshelf, which was lined with countless books on self-development, mindset and spirituality. Turns out … she didn't do it alone. She had the world's best mentors at her fingertips and she was dedicated to learning everything she could from them.

She had committed herself to sparking positive change in her life. She had set herself a goal to read one hundred self-development books in a year, which she said was not easy to start as she wasn't a keen reader, but she persisted and mixed it up with audio books so she could listen on the go. Over this time, she absorbed critical information on hacking her happiness, life tools for breaking old habits and thought patterns, shifting her mindset, being conscious of the cause of her frustrations … it was endless, and things began to change. She healed from old emotional wounds, forgave people she thought she would never forgive and found her true self and purpose. Then opportunities started coming her way and the cloud started to clear.

I too was thirsty to make change, and up until that moment I hadn't known how on earth I would even start. I ripped a corner off one of the production sheets I had used for the shoot day and asked her to write down one book that she suggested I read first to help me find more clarity and peace in my life.

It was then my pathway to purpose started. I downloaded that first book, which happened to be by Dr Joe Dispenza, titled *Breaking the Habit of Being Yourself*. How fitting.

Over the next several years I was on a mission to absorb and learn. I wanted to be happier. I wanted to be the parent and wife I had always dreamt of, and I wanted to smash my career dreams! I read book after book, did courses, attended retreats, found like-minded people, consumed podcasts … the more I could take in, the better. And slowly I started to see positive changes within myself, my beliefs and my behaviour that began to filter out to my husband and kids.

The more I learnt, the more I started to see things differently.

At this time my husband and I had been having a few crappy years as a couple, we were disconnected and on different wavelengths. He was working excessively, travelling two to three days a week, tired, moody, frustrated—we were like ships in the night and barely connected even when we were together.

As he saw changes in me, he slowly started becoming interested in the books I was reading too and started his own journey of self-discovery. In those few years we both became new people. It was a truly amazing transition of our marriage. We felt like we saw each other clearly for the first time in a very long time, because we were clearer on who we were as individuals. People would often see us together and comment on how different we seemed.

I know for certain, had it not been for us doing this work on ourselves, we would not be together today.

I realised that interviewing that single mum on that shoot day was a truly life-changing moment that altered the trajectory of my life. It was that way because I decided it would be. I knew things were only going to get worse if I didn't change and instead of hitting rock bottom mentally, emotionally and physically, I decided to consciously create change.

I began to wonder what other new life experiences could change the way I felt and behaved.

A couple of years after that shoot day, I was asked by a mentor to list twenty five life-defining moments, no matter how big or small, that had happened throughout the course of my life, even in childhood. I hadn't thought of looking into the past to determine what experiences were perhaps shaping my current behaviour and what triggered me. When my mentor asked me this, I instantly thought that I surely didn't have that many life-altering moments from my past! I had lived an apparently normal life and there were perhaps one to two things I could think of that affected the way I lived my life.

But once I started putting pen to paper, things started flowing; experiences, memories and conversations started coming to me— even from when I was ten years old, right up to the present moment— that I still played over in my head, even one-off comments that I believed to be true about myself and the world. I began to realise these experiences may still be influencing the way I was reacting to life. And I wanted to dive deeper into creating a new perspective that was actually and fully my own.

In late 2020, my little family decided it was time for more change. My husband had recently quit a twenty-year career in property, I was working remotely on my businesses and we had nothing tying us down to Australia. We had a rare chance to take this opportunity. We knew that to redefine ourselves fully and become who we wanted to be, we needed to get out of the environment we were in.

We rented out our house fully furnished, packed all of our clothes and important belongings into nine suitcases and headed off to the tropical oasis of Fiji, which had a population of eight hundred and fifty thousand people.

I had never imagined myself choosing to live the island life. As a city girl, I yearned for people, busyness, the fast pace, bright lights … I had always imagined if I ever got the courage to move that it would be to somewhere like NYC, Hong Kong or Singapore. But the way the world was in its current state, that was not meant to be, and our destiny led us here.

Many of our friends and family thought we were completely mad, packing up our lives in the middle of a pandemic to move to a third-world country, with absolutely no plans. We had placed our bets on the universe to show us the way forward. It was so exciting and new … we had never done this before.

When we arrived in Fiji, we felt instant freedom. Not only because we were away from COVID restrictions in Melbourne—we had endured eight months of strict lockdowns over 2020—but because we were truly proud of feeling the fear of this huge change, and doing it anyway. It was liberating.

As we met new people, I instantly saw the difference in how we introduced ourselves. Because my husband and I had changed so significantly in the past few years, having done so much self-work, we felt free enough to speak as that new person to people we met. We were more open and felt free to be whomever we wanted to be.

When you change, it is hard for people around you, who have known you so long, to accept that. A lot of people don't like change, it makes them uncomfortable, so they steer away from it. We were doing the opposite and choosing change, and it felt great.

There is a drawing I saw recently that shows a caterpillar and butterfly. The caterpillar says to the butterfly, 'You've changed,' and the butterfly says, 'We are supposed to.' I smiled when I saw that, as it resonated so deeply with me. I was proud of the changes we had made, individually, as a couple and as a family, and I knew we were where we were meant to be.

The other amazing thing about moving your life with only limited possessions is that you learn to simplify your lifestyle. I began to realise that 'things' are not what makes me happy; it is experiences and special moments that create the best memories. I realised that pushing myself into discomfort and the unknown—and away from the security of my network in Australia—created so much opportunity for growth and exploration. There was so much more self-reliance and independence in my new life being away from home and it opened up a whole other part of me.

When I look at the photo taken of me on the day I left Australia, I feel like I am a different person with a new outlook. A person with more courage, new dreams, crazy goals and more clarity.

I am not a person who has gone through crazy highs and lows in life. I did not hit rock bottom before deciding to create great change. I have chosen to find moments that inspired me to grow, little events and signs that triggered me into realising that if I didn't make adjustments to the way I thought and behaved, that huge rock-bottom moment would most definitely come knocking.

There are Japanese concepts called 'kensho' and 'satori' I have become very fond of, and I feel encapsulates a lot of how I feel about conscious change. It defines two pathways of growth. Kensho is a pathway of pain—a huge moment in your life that is triggered by a significant painful event, which forces you to take action. Satori, on the other hand, are inspired moments and realisations that weave a pathway to change—this can perhaps be slower but is of course much less painful.

I am driven to share this story so that more people consciously choose 'satori' or inspired pathways—as I have done—to avoid the huge trauma, heartache and pain, and pick up on those small moments in which we notice that things need to shift. Those little hints or nudges from the universe that will lead you gently in a new direction.

Sometimes it is not easy opening ourselves up to share our personal struggles and experiences, but we share our stories in the hope that they can help others; even reading this journey may be an inspired moment in itself for you to make change, to change the job you have disliked for the last ten years, to shift your unhealthy lifestyle habits that are no longer serving you, to end friendships that have been toxic for too long or relationships that aren't working—or simply start doing more of the things that bring you joy, and less of the things that don't.

I hope that sharing my story helps you to create the life you want to live, take action to live purposefully and truly see yourself for the beautiful soul that you are.

# About the author

# Maritza Barone

Maritza Barone is a presenter and producer whose mission is to elevate people who are using their voices to push humanity forward, through the content she creates and is involved in.

In 2019, Maritza co-founded Conscious Conversations, a company that creates tools and events to enhance human connection. It is the company's aim to create five million genuine and meaningful conversations over the next five years.

In addition to this, Maritza's wellbeing podcast, 'Things You Can't Un-Hear' regularly features in the top fifty self-improvement podcasts in Australia. Maritza interviews leading health and wellness experts, thought leaders and everyday heroes. She is passionate about sharing personal journeys and visions to help people awaken to a higher level of thinking and feed themselves with powerful knowledge that will make the world a better place.

In late 2020, Maritza and her husband, along with their two daughters, decided it was time to follow their dreams of living abroad.

They packed their lives into nine suitcases and headed to live the island life in Fiji. Even with no plans, mid-pandemic, they knew in their hearts the move was what they needed to change and grow. Returning to Australia almost a year later, their experience of relocating created an undeniable bond within their family. They proved to themselves they had the courage to make bold decisions for positive life change.

**www.maritzabarone.com**

*Maritza is currently running sessions with corporate teams, individuals and groups on the Power of Voice, where she helps people to find and share their unique voice.*

# 7.

# A path in the dark

## MELANIE TONGMAR

I began writing this chapter thinking that I would write about the potential of humans as intuitive beings. Drawing from my own experience as someone guided mainly by intuition, I was reflecting on how following our inner voice can be challenging amidst the cultural noise, and ways I have overcome that. It was an okay chapter, though it danced merrily on the surface of intimacy, without any real juice.

But during the final weeks of fleshing out this chapter, three things happened that pulled that flesh from the bone:

- I was given a dire medical prognosis, which has required me to completely overhaul the way I have been living, and quickly.
- I have been given the gut-wrenching news that one of my sweetest and dearest friends does not have much time left on this earth.
- I fell into one of the darkest nights of my soul, a darkness that I have not experienced for a very long time.

Suddenly, the superfluous was cut from my life and very quickly I reached ground zero. I have had to hold space for myself and sit through these experiences with a grieving heart.

So this story is raw. It is not a 'how to', nor does it have a pointed, obvious truth shared with you in a 'teaching moment'. Instead, I have gone back to my lived experience and the things that have helped me on this path, embracing fear while I step forward into the untraversed terrain of publicly sharing something so precious and intimate.

I have my beliefs, my bone-deep knowing of what I have experienced as truth. But, like you, I hold within me the wisdom and fallibility of being human, of my ancestry, of social conditioning and the way I was raised. Extracting our truth from a conditioned life can be quite an unravelling, and it begins with our stories.

My story is one of persistent spiritual, psychological and emotional self-inquiry and a lifelong stormy search for self. My story is a dance between trying to function within the constraints and prejudices of the dominant cultural narrative and remembering the ways of my ancestors, of belonging to the earth, of the stars, the plants, the animals, and the wandering spirits of this world and others. It's a story not of an unwavering Truth, but of how I have coped with the human experience and the beliefs that have anchored and propelled me in a discordant, spiralling dance of self-realisation.

In my more mystical experiences, I've flown through space, disembodied, a gaseous nothing. I've been in contact with beings from other galaxies, had surgery performed by star people, walked through my dreams into the waking life of others, and spoken with loved ones long dead and gone. I've felt the orgasmic rapture of oneness, of complete surrender to the cosmos, where I dissolved into pure energy. I've felt the dark magic of my ancestors, the bloody vacuous depths sucking at my soul. I've heard animals 'talk' to me, seen wavering, nebulous holographic colours emanating from a tree and felt the power source of the earth through my bare feet. However, I don't place these occurrences on an altar of supernatural, psychic fluency, because I believe these kinds of experiences are actually native to the human experience, just like breathing.

The first time I consciously experienced something more than my physical self, I was six years old. I remember it clearly. I was in kindergarten, and all the other children were on one side of the room, playing 'mums and dads' or 'house', something like that, engrossed in the mimicry that children enjoy as they learn how to be in the world. I sat, in brown corduroy pants and striped t-shirt, sporting a bowl cut, on the other side of the room. Just watching them play, feeling a little separate somehow. All of a sudden, what they were doing made no sense to me. Pouring tea. Tucking the dolls into bed. 'Honey, I'm home!' and 'How was your day, Dear?' I felt like I was observing strange alien rituals and ceremonies I couldn't understand; they seemed so puzzling.

My teacher, Mrs Blacker (with her kind eyes) came over and asked if I wanted to play with some plasticine. I snapped out of my trance, and immediately my heart bubbled. 'Yes, please,' I said.

For the rest of the afternoon, Mrs Blacker allowed me my own space in the corner of the classroom. I sat on a yellow plastic chair with the plasticine, moulding and shaping it. The other children eventually sat back down on the front mat and did their singing, lessons and games, but Mrs Blacker let me be all by myself.

By the end of the afternoon, Mrs Blacker came over and asked how I was doing. I showed her, with beaming pride, my magnum opus.

It was a crudely sculptured frog.

Now, this kindergarten was in Melbourne in 1981. Malcolm Fraser was the Prime Minister of Australia, we sang *God Save the Queen*, and the repercussions of the Vietnam War were still reverberating across the globe. So far, I'd lived a somewhat beatnik, middle-class city life: asphalt and ashrams, smog, skyscrapers, trams and dingy alleys, grown-ups sneaking cheeky joints in the backyard, political rallies, metal playgrounds, and kicking old empty cigarette packets amongst the puffy autumn leaves piling along the street drains.

But, at that moment, at almost six years old, as I was pressing the plasticine between my fingers, something new came to me. A warm, glowing sensation enveloped my head, then expanded down through my heart and out of my hands. Something independent of me, not from the city, not from my little world. I wasn't at all afraid. I was engaged in artistic oblivion. I was in the zone, and it felt *right*.

Mrs Blacker was so proud of me. She took a photo of me with my plasticine frog as I worked away intently and with complete focus. She had recognised my need for solitude and, perhaps unknowingly, nurtured my connection to something more considerable than me in that moment. It all felt so natural, though, and I may have forgotten the incident had I not kept that photo.

A vast collection of unusual experiences like this have punctuated my life. Some are more gentle, some more intense, more initiatory. Some are momentary, some have lasted weeks, months, years. I never sought them. They just happened and, as I tried to unfurl and understand, my experiences deepened. The more entrenched I became in the conditioning of others, the more often they were a dark, soul-wrenching, disembodied unravelling. But now, having lived from age six to nearly half a century, that unfurling is a more conscious process. I have learnt to sit in these spaces and offer myself grace to move through them, observing with curious compassion, the wise mind watching the watcher.

It was not long after the plasticine frog incident that, for various reasons, my parents decided to pack up the rusty Nissan van, leave the big smoke and head north to Byron Bay (back then a small, sleepy coastal town with a few shops, a school and a pub).

We had little in the way of money and spent the first few years living in a shed where we had purchased a parcel of land—treeless and overgrazed—not really knowing how much work it would be to restore it to rainforest, nor how much this land would change us ... how much it would change me and become part of my identity.

Over the next few years, my parents gifted my brother and me with many pets: a little goat named Frank, Poppy the Jersey calf, several chickens (all named) and three beautiful dogs in succession. I adored the animals, and we took it upon ourselves to take care of them as they lived and also as they died. My brother and I spent much time running around nude in the sunshine with muddy feet. I felt a special connection to the land and the animals, our lives intertwined, and I settled into this way of being in the world.

Despite the beauty around us, and though we were a close-knit, open-minded family with solid values and a pioneering spirit, my childhood was also one marked by volatility. My father—clever, charismatic, an artist, a poet, a philosopher—struggled with the considerable challenges of being an Asian man in rural White Australia. In his isolation and loneliness, I became my father's focus— his protégé and confidant held hostage to his pain. As a family, we were the captive audience who witnessed both his playful exuberance and explosive rage.

These violent incidents blew up larger than life in my heart and naturally, as a sensitive child, I became anxious and hypervigilant. I learnt to read energy and body language very well, and my already-strong empathetic nature became even more heightened. I learnt how to walk on eggshells. I learnt that I was responsible for how other people felt and that it was my duty to be emotionally available to everyone, a dumping ground for other people's pain, even when those experiences left me crumbling in on myself.

Feeling everything with critically poor boundaries is a recipe for disaster. I grew up emotionally enmeshed with other people's suffering. I accepted violent and inappropriate breaches, even when they made me feel physically sick, and began victim shaming myself. I began constantly overthinking and over-analysing other people's behaviour and responses (something I still struggle with occasionally). Everything I did was premeditated and aligned just so to ensure the safest possible outcome and keep me from harm. I became an empty room with an open door, where people came to dump their stuff. And some of that stuff was heavy. And I didn't recognise it was other people's stuff! I thought it was mine to bear, and that there was something wrong with me because being alive wasn't fun. It felt heavy and exhausting. I knew that I was not coping with life as easily as most kids seemed to be. I wanted so much to feel light, but I didn't know how.

I developed compulsive and unhealthy habits—overworking, over-achieving, over-giving and overeating, and in my late teens befriending amphetamines for a few years to keep up with my hypervigilance. My only healthy refuges were music, reading, writing and art making—painting and drawing my happy place of expression. I sketched the beings who visited me in my dreams and from other earthly realms and galaxies. I painted quiet pictures of my own body, split open, with all my insides displayed for the world to see. My art was in secret. My art was for me.

Sometime after my formative years, at about seventeen, I was browsing through Noah's Ark, my favourite esoteric bookstore, where I discovered a small, unobtrusive brown book that intrigued me. The tiny title, embossed in gold: *Earth Magic: A Dianic book of shadows* by Marion Weinstein. An electric current shot through my spine, my hair stood on end as I rifled through the pages … and thus began a twenty-year relationship with Celtic witchcraft and earth magic.

Over the years, I spent more and more scattered time practising my craft, a solitary witchling, learning about my Celtic heritage and ancestry, developing rituals and ceremonies around the sun, the moon, the cycles and elements in the natural world around me. I was introduced to the concept of boundaries in a magical, energetic way, though not in a practical day-to-day way through human interaction (there was not much, if any, easily accessible information on this in the early nineties). Through the study of witchcraft, I became adept at the art of glamouring and shapeshifting—making myself appear as something I was not. Manipulating how people saw me, being whomever they needed me to be to protect myself and survive.

I grew comfortable in the shadows with my masks. Still, although I held an ongoing reverence and awe for the earth's beauty and had become quietly confident in my art, that clawing darkness kept returning, over and over in pulsating, rhythmic consistency. Round and round. Up and down. Exaltation and agony. Death and rebirth.

The earth became the nest that held me in my darkest moments. I began to surrender to the peace and stillness I experienced there. The land was my home that nurtured my spirit, and I felt her whispers and her rhythmic cycles reflected in me. The murmuring below the mountain. The frenzy of the storm. The blush of a flower petal and the burn of fire. Birth and death. And throughout it all, a thrumming vibration that connected everything. I was in my early thirties, and so ready for change.

Seeing the beauty in the earth and all her aspects—gentle and nurturing, destructive and wild—I began to see that beauty echoed within myself. I had a committed relationship with ritual and ceremony, working closely with the goddess Cerridwen (still my goddess of choice), yet slowly I relinquished my fervent grip on my practice.

There was something bigger here, and it was simply the earth beneath my feet and the sky above my head. The Great Mother, cradling me in all my perceived brokenness. Never judging. Always listening. Giving me space to just be.

The earth hummed. Harmonious. Whispering. Colours heightened. I felt and occasionally saw the energetic, ectoplasmic fields that encase each living being—the trees, the air, the soil, the animals, including things some may consider non-living: rocks, water, sticks, bones—the fields expanding and contracting in communion.

And suddenly, nature was not something 'out there'. It was a part of me. The forest and the sky were a part of me in a way that can only be experienced in kinship.

In reverence, I began to paint every day. I still couldn't be open about how I saw the world; instead, I painted it. Abstract riots of colour and shapes, nothing defined, nothing physically recognisable, but I painted the spirit I felt. Painting became my language, my release, and I surrendered to the process. I sold quite a few artworks through galleries and stores over the years and even had an exhibition. I felt liberated in that embodied experience. I could show people what I felt, what I saw, without saying a word. That's why I believe creativity is a language of the universe, and we, as artists of our lives, are channels and vessels of that.

I found rhythm and revelation in dark nights of the soul, and I found myself always being drawn to those moments of transition, of the horizon's edge—the birth of my son, assisting others in giving birth, sitting with the dying and those in spiritual crisis. These profound experiences of vulnerability, of finite human life, propelled me to drop the masks and to roll up my sleeves and do the work—to speak true, nurture my inner child, reparent myself, hold myself safe, and maintain robust boundaries.

And finally, I forgave myself. This act was a massive turning point, adding a lightness of being to my life. Since then, holding the tension of light and dark, yin and yang, birth and death, love and fear, hope and hopelessness—being able to contain duality in integrated wholeness has been part of my practice.

This truth of me, this snippet of my story, of meeting myself after all those years has been quite a journey. The path has been challenging, but it has been the unavoidable step-by-step journey towards my own healing, my ability to hold compassion and courage for others, and my remembrance of being part of something greater than myself. In this journey that is ongoing, I reclaim my inner hero and inner child, my sage, my priestess, and I find my seat of self-sovereignty. I am very comfortable in the uncomfortable dark places because I know my map of that experience well, and I know that with great darkness comes the potential of great light. I have surrendered to my uncertainty, my unknowing of The Great Mystery.

As I reflect, writing these words, I can now see how magnificent I am in just being here. How magnificent we all are. We are not a rose bloomed from a single bud. We each are our own garden, with a rich variety of trees, plants, fungi, flowers, animals, devas and deities, habitats, and weather patterns … an ecosystem within ourselves. A world within reflecting into the world without.

Some days we may struggle through the storm. Other days we fly free through the trees, flourishing in our private paradise, aware that the dark, the night, the shadow places also belong here.

It's not always easy, but I lovingly tend to that garden, and am at peace on the horizon's edge. To live in the dawn and the twilight— like you, perhaps, recovering those liminal places of existence within, in the ether, in the forest places, in art, poetry and dreams. This is an ancient way of being, a human way of being, a relevant and necessary reclamation of being that requires a place in the future we are creating. It's time to expand the story of what it actually means to be human.

So this I know is true—for me. Our truth lies within own stories, and our life experience is what makes us already whole. Anything that doesn't feel resolved, or comfortable, or is painful, is a part of that completeness, even as we may strive for something different. We are not on a path to something better or higher or even other than what we are.

We are simply unfolding into ourselves.

*I pay my respects to the original custodians of this land, past, present, and emerging. I reside in Nyangbal country in the Bundjalung Nation and acknowledge this land was never ceded. Living with this land greatly informs my own identity and spiritual practice, and I endeavour to continue my own education of Indigenous people, their stories, histories and traditional and ongoing culture so that I may be more ethical and inclusive in my work and in my life.*

# About the author

# Melanie Tongmar

Melanie Tongmar is a transpersonal life coach and spiritual emergence guide, who's joy lies in exploring and integrating the fundamental medicine pathways of Ancestral Ways, Nature Kinship, Creative Play and Mindfulness back into our ways of being. The passion she brings to her work stems from a lifelong fascination with the human condition and our connection to the world, including the liminal and mystical aspects that go beyond the physical self.

Melanie comes from a lineage of Thai spirit doctors and Celtic ancestors who are a vital source of wisdom in her work with people going through transitions, energetic shifts, experiencing divergent ways of being, and searching for their own true nature. She firmly believes that with integrated aspects of self, and a revitalisation of a relational way of being, we can live a life with more ease, more meaning, compassion and deeper connection, and find our way back home to ourselves.

www.melanietongmar.com

# 8.

# The secret club

## ALEXANDRA WIATR

**July 2019**

The fresh July rain splatters gently onto the windshield, droplets of water sparkling in the night. The windshield wipers hum away in the background, whisking droplets off the glass as soon as they appear. The glimmer of the night sky reflects off the dark pavement and I notice just how eerily quiet the outside world is around me.

I gaze wistfully—emptily, rather—past the stoplights in front of me. I'm two minutes from home, on my way back from running a few evening errands while Aidan looks after Aurora.

I can't remember the last time I drove a car by myself. Was it before giving birth earlier this year in January, perhaps? I can't remember the last time it was just me and my thoughts, alone and uninterrupted. This stolen moment of quiet time—this momentary spaciousness in the repetitive sea that can be motherhood—should be cause for celebration. I should be welcoming this peace and space, this down time to ponder my musings as I please.

But this isn't the quiet I crave.

And tonight, there are no musings.

There haven't been any musings, actually, for what feels like a very long time.

The feeling creeps in again. Or rather, I'm finally in the quiet, which allows me to notice it.

It's always there, really, these days. This feeling, with its black, sticky, muddy tar-like wrath, oozing and seeping throughout every inch of my body. Pulling me down and sucking me in, deep into its black-hole-like abyss. The feeling that zaps the life and joy and energy right from my very being, leaving me wrung out and dry until there's nothing left to feel.

Because that's how it feels these days ... like there's nothing left to feel.

I gaze hollowly out of the window and wonder to myself, *When was the last time I felt joy? When was the last time I felt true, pure, radiating gratitude? It used to come so easily to me.*

*Will I ever feel lively—truly alive—again? Will there ever come a day where it doesn't feel like I'm simply going through the motions, ticking the boxes off an endless list of mundane chores, until it's time for bed again?*

The light turns green and right on cue, my right foot presses the accelerator. I turn left onto Greenhill Road and the mist from the freshly rained-on pavement rises up from my tires as I round my turn. I look up and see it—an eighteen-wheel semi truck hurtling toward me in the opposite lane.

*You know,* says a voice inside my head, *you could just drive right into it and end this misery right now.* Tears fill my eyes as I briefly and very genuinely consider.

The night sky seems to swallow me whole at the very thought.

What would it feel like, to die like that? Would it hurt? Physically, I mean. Would it be quick? One swift right turn of my steering wheel and I could soon find out, if I wanted to. The truck looks like it's driving fast enough for me to be zapped from this life upon impact.

Time stands still as my thoughts come to a slow, contemplative halt.

Is that what I want? To be zapped from this life?

I begin to imagine my body lying crumpled and listless on the pavement, our silver Ford Focus scattered in a million pieces. I see my soul, a shimmering cloudy mist, leave my body, gazing at the world around as she rises above. Everything from this vantage point looks so … peaceful. So still.

Aurora's sweet little six-month-old cherub face instantly fills my mind; she stares up at me with her soft, plush cheeks and toothless baby smile, eyes full of love and wonder. As my soul begins to rise further and further away from my lifeless body, I see our little home from a bird's eye view. How perfect and quaint it looks from here … how have I never noticed its picturesque serenity until now?

As I float further away from Earth, I see my beautiful Aurora growing up without a mother, confused and sad about why she was never enough to keep me going. I see my husband crying in anguish, alone at night as he wonders how he—how anyone—could have missed the signs that I wasn't well. I see the bits and pieces of our life, of our hopes and dreams that could have been but never were, flicker across a slow and grainy camera reel.

*Fuck.*

I jolt myself back to reality as the semi truck passes by. That isn't what I want. Deep down, of course I know that. But lately, it's so hard to decipher what's true and what's just fog. I pluck myself from one twisted and altered version of my mind's reality and into a new reality, the one where my soul resides.

But my soul … she's been so quiet these past few months. Where are you, inspiration? Are you hiding somewhere, purpose? Sense of wonder and awe seems to be missing altogether, there's no trace of her anywhere. And what in the hell has anyone done with my love and zest for life?

What are these thoughts? And where are they coming from? More importantly, why can't I stop thinking and feeling them? Will I ever make it out of this fog? Will I ever feel truly, deeply, radiantly alive again?

All I know is that the only thing that makes me feel alive these days is holding my baby. My sweet, sweet, perfect and soft baby. The one who makes me feel complete and whole and so *alive* like never before. The one who fills the gaping hole in my belly—a gaping hole that has only existed since giving birth six months ago. I feel empty now when I'm not with her. The world doesn't make sense anymore when it's just me alone in it.

Of course Aurora is enough. She will always be. I make a mental note to hold her tight when I get home and whisper gently into her ear, *You will always be enough for me, my little darling.*

But deep down, no matter how strongly I know my child will always be more than enough for the woman and mother I have now become, I also know I want more than that—I need more than this— to feel whole again. As much as it haunts me to admit it, motherhood alone isn't enough for the woman I am meant to be.

And then the guilt pours in for even feeling this way in the first place.

So what am I to do? Where am I to go from here?

*You know where,* whispers a soft voice within. My body recoils at this knowing. The road ahead ... what I know that voice is telling me to do ... is so terrifying. So unknown. Where that voice is telling me to go, and the things I know I'll need to do to get there, feel so far away.

Deep down, I know first and foremost I need to tell Aidan what has just happened. Although it all occurred in a split second, I know I can't leave out any detail, any feeling. I know I'm going to need his help if I'm to make it through this and emerge safely on the other side.

It's going to feel uncomfortable, it's going to feel stretchy. But I have to do it now, while the feelings are still fresh within my body.

I swallow the air around me and continue my drive home.

## May 2020

'Breathe into it,' he says.

My entire body tenses up as my energy healer guides me back to the place I used to be. I try to resist going back with every fibre of my being as I lie on my bed and listen to his voice. I don't want to go there ... back to that place of bleak darkness and spiralling despair. I've come so far ... done so much work both inside and out ... and yet ... here it is. Back again, pulling me down and sucking me under, just like the quicksand I remember it to be.

Just as I allow that rock-bottom feeling to overcome me—the same one I felt that rainy evening of the oncoming semi truck nearly one year ago—a gentle voice emerges from within.

*Release it*, she says. *You're safe now.*

I breathe in, gathering every droplet of despair from the depths of my body, holding them there for a moment or two. I allow the stickiness to overcome me, breathing in deeper as I feel my chest begin to tighten. Just as I feel the darkness begin to envelop me once again, I open my lips and exhale more deeply than I ever have before.

I feel the darkness leave my body as the last drop of breath escapes my lips. A crash of white light floods in and I'm transported to a time and place in the future.

There we are, the three of us standing together before a beautiful, majestic home. The sky above is a brilliant shade of blue and the old, wise trees surrounding us whisper gently in the soft summer breeze. In the distance we hear the ocean waves crash into the shore.

Aidan holds Aurora's hand—she's young still, about three and certainly not more than four—as the two of them skip toward the front door. I stand back a little as I pause in awe to admire the beauty and wonder of what we've created in such a short time. I place my hand on my belly and notice that I'm pregnant again. Quite pregnant, actually, perhaps due any day.

My current self holds this vision for a moment or two longer, its symbolism not lost on me. It's been nearly one year since that life-changing moment, driving in the rain down Greenhill Road, and our lives have almost completely transformed since then.

In one short year, Aidan and I have laid the foundations of a business together, one born from the depths of the darkness I experienced and he helped me through. One born from our hearts, a beautiful blend of technology and spirit. A business we can operate from any corner of the world, one that has opened doors we never imagined. One that, just this very month, has set us both free from working for someone else. We turned the depths of that darkness into light, creating a life where family and work and play all intertwine as one.

The scene of my vision changes and suddenly a portal surrounded by a ring of fire opens up at my feet. I'm standing just before its opening, holding Aurora on my hip as we peer inside. Her soft, snuggly body melts into mine in that familiar way and as I look into her eyes, a soft, expectant smile begins to spread across her little cherub face. The flames from the portal lick our feet, but they don't feel like fire. Instead they feel warm and welcoming, inviting us in.

'Now what?' I ask my healer as my vision self brings Aurora a little tighter against my body.

'Go into it,' he says, and I can tell he is grinning.

Aurora and I look at each other, smiling. Into the unknown we go.

**Present day**

If there is one thing I know now, it is that darkness is meant to be felt, not feared. For it is resisting the darkness that creates the tension.

It's so counterintuitive. But after all, we're human. Designed and created to feel a big, whole, wide range of emotions. It's true, some are more pleasant than others. But what this dance with anxiety in motherhood has taught me is that we cannot turn the dial down on one set of emotions without turning the dial down on all. Working to eliminate the sticky emotions can be temporary relief in the short term, but in time, such a way of being—feeling—cuts us off from experiencing the joy. The radiance. The bliss.

It's safe to feel them, my dear. It is safe to feel all of your emotions.

There's one other thing too. One big thing that I wish more women shouted from the rooftops, and it's this: we don't lose the essence of our selves when we become a mother.

It's true, we shed. We grow. We learn. Some days we feel indescribable wonder and wholeness, others we feel as though we've been chewed up and spat back out by the task that is giving our minds, bodies and souls fully and completely to the little souls that once grew within our very bones.

But this phase of life doesn't have to be a departure from who we truly are. In fact, I've come to prefer the term 'evolution'. After all, isn't that a bit like life? Isn't that the whole cycle of things within and around us, really? That nothing is ever really gone … it just grows.

And we, as women and mothers, are just the same. The maidens within us still exist, playful and innocent, fiery and sexy. Alive. They've simply journeyed to the heavens and back to bring our beautiful children earthside, and transformed and grown wise along the way like never before. Unable to go back but also not yearning to, because to do so would be to give up so much, not just as mothers, but as women.

And I suppose there is one final thing, the best-kept secret of all. The thing no one can ever tell you, because you have to believe it for yourself first: that you can do anything as a woman.

You can *especially* do anything as a mother.

This, above all, I know is true.

# About the author

# Alexandra Wiatr

Alexandra is a wife, mama, and multi-passionate woman on a mission to show mothers everywhere the infinite possibility that comes along with motherhood. From the ashes of her mental wellness breakdown in 2019, Alexandra and her husband turned an idea on their living room couch into what will become a 7-figure business by 2022. Alexandra is now carving out a new niche in the 'maiden to mother' narrative, guiding mamas to connect to their sensuality to unlock their most abundant lives. Alexandra and her family live freely and happily in Perth, West Australia. Her vision from May 2020 did, in fact, come true and she & Aidan are expecting their second baby just months after Aurora's 3rd birthday.

# 9.

# We are not broken

## LARINA TIFFEN-FULLER

*We are not broken.*
*We don't need to be fixed.*
*We just need to give ourselves permission to remember and honour parts of ourselves that we have forgotten.*
*We need to reclaim and honour who we are and who we came here to be!*
*And part of that is owning everything we were told we couldn't be.*
*We were taught to fear, to not own our darkness, the parts of ourselves that others could not see, feel, sense or understand.*
*It's in our history through the stories, myths, and gospel that is retold to keep us suppressed.*
*It doesn't make it true, it does not make it right, it's been built on false lies, to make us not whole.*

Well, I am calling bullshit on that, as now is the time.

We must heal what is not broken but in fact pure and true.
Now is the time we must give ourselves greater permission to step forward.

Women are being called forward to honour who we are, and be part of the collective energy to heal, to co-create this new portal we are entering.

We can no longer hide behind the veil as it's becoming thinner by the day.

We no longer can ignore what we feel or see, or what is rising within us.

We can't keep trying to fit in, to make others comfortable.

We must clear years of suppression and stop trying to fit into the system, an ideal, a belief of what we must be to be accepted, rather than who we are.

For me, this light activation has been an ongoing process of mini light-bulb moments, breadcrumbs leading me closer to self, SHE, where I have been forced to take notice. I have been raw, soaked in fear and in a fetal position on the cold bathroom floor. And this vulnerability is allowing me to get closer to her, my wise women, my sovereign women, my divine self that's been calling me from within. Banging at the door.

This led me to moments of greater understanding, awareness, as nothing in my logical mind made sense of it, but I knew it to be true.

I know it's within me and beyond me. And its knowledge I wish to share. I didn't wake up one day and decide I was spiritual, or awakened. It's been a part of me for a very long time.

### Sacred Share—My story

As I lay in the hospital bed waiting on the anaesthetist, a part of me started thinking, *God, I am not even forty, in fact I am two weeks away, and I have a cataract over my right eye.* I thought that was an old person's disease. Truth be said, I may not be old in this lifetime, but I am an old soul. I wonder if this is a sacred contract that I have carried into this lifetime ... I breathed out a sigh.

Then *What if?* crept in!

What if I never see my son get married, see his first day at school, meet his girlfriend, watch him go to prom, meet my grandchild ... what if it all goes horribly wrong?

The women beside the nearby bed had seen all that. I may not.

I could feel the panic overcome my body and start flooding through every part of my being.

A part of me had surrendered, as deep within me I knew this day was coming. I wanted it, if the truth be said. Just not as loud of what my physical body had manifested.

I wanted to be activated, to step into this side of myself and own what I was hiding from the world.

I wanted to show up as the Real me, not the fake one you see.

But I was scared; what if no one understood me, or they made fun of me, or did not believe me?

Centuries ago, women were burnt for owning this part of their internal self, the knowing, seeing. This pain still runs through my body, as I was once ridiculed, stoned, beaten, naked, left vulnerable there to burn, and it is the part I needed to heal.

As I lay there overthinking, going round and round in circles, my breath started to get shallow. I felt like I couldn't breathe into the pit of my stomach, like it had all of a sudden become hollow. A tear rolled down my cheek.

Why was I so scared to own ME! The part that gave me the greatest joy, completed me wholeheartedly, and was part of my authenticity and my magic in this world. The part that never failed;

it always showed up when I had the courage to ask, and had deeply supported me through times of great fear and struggle.

Then she appeared in my mind's eye, standing beside me as if I had summoned her, and called my name so softly. Anna—my best friend since high school.

*Hard up, I had worse operations than this.*

And I smiled and laughed as she was right.

In that moment, a complete calmness and light took over my body.

Next, she spoke to me the words I was not ready to hear, at a physical level: Let alone witness within me 'What parts of yourself are you not allowing people to see?'

All of me! She was right, I was only allowing people to see one aspect of me, the safe, accepted side that fits into society and gets invited to social gatherings.

Anna was that sister you could tell anything to and know that she wouldn't need to understand or fix it, she just held that space for you. She knew my inner power as a medium, witch and priestess because she had experienced it alongside me, all through our years together growing up.

I would finish her sentences, know when she was sad or mad, feel her ask for me or think of me, and I would call. She was the first person I had the courage to read for, channel for, and she saw me.

We were connected beyond something physical.

She died of cancer two weeks before I went completely blind in my right eye.

I knew she was dying; I had felt it weeks before she knew. Deep in the night I was awoken by a deep knowing that I couldn't shift, drenched in sweat, crying—I rolled over to look at the clock and saw it 3.13am—bloody angel hour!

This feeling, knowing, sixth sense, it had happened many times before and I knew this time it was different. I no longer could push down nor run and hide from these feelings anymore.

Like other times before.

I couldn't speak to them for fear of it manifesting itself.

And once you know what you know, you can't forget that knowing.


For weeks it haunted me, like a cloud of darkness.

And I just sat with it, not speaking because I didn't want to give it a voice. Grieving, the unknown knowing.

Then one day my phone rang, and as I reached for it after the third ring, I knew this was the phone call that would change not only my life but also the life of the person at the other end.

Six weeks later I lost my best friend.

Two weeks later I was fully blind in one eye, not even forty!

And here I am ... Needing to make change, needing to acknowledge, needing to forgive, needing to heal.


The little girl in me knew at a very early age I was different by the look Mum and Dad would give each other when I spoke my truth. And when I told people my truth, they would tell me I was a liar, call me names and hurt me, so I learnt to lie, tell little white tales, but never my truth.

My mum would always say, *You're away with the fairies*, and yes, she was right. It was easy for me to be in my internal world and show up as who I really was and how I felt in this world.

At the time of my first encounter with spirit, I didn't know what was happening. And I thought that everyone around me could see, feel and hear what I could.

Looking back now at my four-year-old self, and remembering my first encounter with spirit or something beyond myself, is like recalling something that just happened yesterday.

I was at the Pareora boarding house, playing outside with my sister Haidee, which is what we did most days. We played cowboys and Indians, 'Ring, a Ring, a Rosy'—all the non-PC games that we dare to teach our children nowadays—while our parents and family made lunches for the workers.

And out of nowhere, I heard a male voice speak to me. It felt like it was coming from the sky. I looked up to answer and to see if I could see the man, and in my mind's eye was a man in the sky, an image.

At the time, I didn't know what my mind's eye was as I do now. And I remember in that moment standing still and thinking *This is WAY COOL* and calling Mum and Nanna to come out, trying to hold the image and hear the man still speaking to me.

As soon as I started screaming out 'MUMMMMMM,' the image and the voice drifted away.

Mum came rushing out thinking I was hurt, and I remember saying it didn't matter now the man was gone.

At the time I had no idea what had happened, and not until now, as a forty-year-old woman recalling this childhood memory, I know that this is the truth, my truth as I remember.

This was my first encounter with something or someone outside of this realm, nothing more and nothing less. I don't remember the words spoken, I remember feeling in that moment very invigorated and excited, and I wanted to share it with my mum.

My activation moments came to me as waves in my twenties. This time is when I first encountered angels. I was at a time in my life that was very challenging and confronting, and I was in a lot of emotional pain. Not knowing my next step.

I had just walked out of my marriage to a man deeply loved, but knew in my heart he was never going to change. I had tossed and turned for many years about leaving and when I did, I thought it was going to liberate me. And on some level, it did, as I took back a piece of my inner power.

But here I was six months later, lying in bed and still wondering, *What am I to do?* Still tossing and turning.

This night was no different: the moon was hitting the ocean outside my bedroom window, the sound of the ocean came in and out as I drifted in and out of a conscious state of sleep. Feeling relaxed and still angry at myself for allowing all that was. Praying to my nanna, angels, anyone up there, wherever *there* was, to help me. Give me a sign for fuck's sake! Feeling the ocean flowing within me. Relaxing deeper into my dream state.

Then at the end of my bed appeared a colourful ray of light and magical energy filled the whole room and my body. I felt my soul fill with light and love, that magical feeling you get when you first realise you love someone! You know the feeling when your heart just opens and breathes warmth, and you realise for the first time what love feels like? And it fills your cup and your cup starts overflowing. That was what was happening for me within the four walls of my bedroom.

It was raining pure love and light within me, like I had just been plugged into the universal energy and turned on. All of my unease, despair and pain—about my life, my direction and leaving my marriage—fell away.

I knew in that moment that within myself I would be alright, that I was being guided by something beyond me I couldn't explain.

My energy changed, I changed!

As I fell asleep, I felt held, loved and nourished, knowing that within myself—I've got this!

This thing called life!

I had no plan, no action, but the angels had thrown me the lifeline I needed that night. The next day I cut ties and let go of friendships, pain, loss, broken promises and dreams.

A home that represented so much to me, but then so little. As one chapter was written, I knew not only that I was starting a new chapter but that, in fact, I was the author.

I was claiming and calling back the start of my sovereignty and SHE!


I saw it four years before it happened—didn't know what it was, but I could feel the energy and see people's faces trapped, feeling powerless. I could smell the earth releasing dust and energy. And I saw helicopters in the sky, and I knew it was Kaikoura as the words were being whispered into my ear.

Kaikoura is a seaside township on the south-east coast of New Zealand, an hour and a half away from where I live.

A part of me was too scared to ask, but my heart needed to know, so I asked: *How am I to be of service?*

And the answer was clear: by bringing people together.

I kept this knowing in the back of my mind, in my memory bank, waiting and wondering what it meant and if it would come to fruition. I only told my husband, and family.

Then it began at two past midnight Monday 14 November 2016 as Papatūānuku—Mother Earth—started shaking. Thousands of Kiwis that night were thrown from their bed, into complete darkness and despair. Tsunami sirens rang through the night, as we are taught, if it's strong, get gone. Coastal families evacuated to higher ground, not knowing where they were going or who was hurt or if they were returning. My family came to our home, this was and is our family's plan.

And in that moment, as we embraced each other, we knew not everyone was safe; somewhere in our country we called home, people were not so lucky.

As reports started to come in over the radio, we knew it was north of us.

Waiau, Hanmer Springs, then the words were spoken over the airwaves: no one had contact with Kaikoura. We all looked at each other, and I took a breath.

This was what I had seen. Felt pass through me all those years before.

Was it time for me to show up? Stand in my truth?

I needed to do something, so I asked, *How will you have me be of service?*

Bring people together.

And so I did.

A post on my business Facebook page, Miss Lilly's, asking for baked goods, fresh produce and non-perishable foods, went viral. Over a period of five days, more than two thousand ordinary Kiwis came together to pay it forward. They stood together to support communities isolated by the biggest earthquake in New Zealand history.

How did this happen?

Because I became the vessel. I trusted, surrendered and got out of my own way. I allowed myself to fully step in and be led.

A woman with no money, just pure guidance and trust that resulted in helicopters, aeroplanes, trucks, labour, people, resources, all at my fingertips. That ended in twenty-two tons of food on the HMNZS Canterbury frigate for the people of Kaikoura.

The next breadcrumb came not long after the Kaikoura quake; it played out in my mind's eye like an advertisement for a blockbuster Hollywood movie. A wave of darkness entering the world's atmosphere, and slowly wrapping itself around all the corners of the globe. The energy behind it was fear, sorrow, loss, stillness and death. I remember thinking, *OMG, there is going to be a war.* Truth being said, I had no idea what I was being shown. And when I receive information for the collective, or myself, it sometimes doesn't come to fruition for weeks or years. There is no timeline, as it's not a SMART goal I have set or can control. And when I feel and see what I've been shown, it normally makes no sense. It's like a piece of the jigsaw that sometimes doesn't fit straight away. But the energy it contains and that my body holds while it's passing through me is real. I grieve what I see, get angry, feel powerless, and sense the level of desperation. It's my way of processing the emotion and releasing the vision, but still banking it in my memory for future understanding.

In December 2019, the dark cloud had arrived. And I remember watching the news: Wuhan, China. The first wave of darkness had started, I was told. What we now know as COVID-19 has impacted and made its presence known to every citizen of the world.

I said to my husband as we watched the news, 'Here it is, that's coming here. The world is about to become very still.'

I was in the midst of wedding season with Miss Lilly's, my catering company. It was our biggest season to date. As we entered January, then February, borders were starting to close, and so were people's dreams of coming back to New Zealand to get married. Cancellations started rolling in. Email after email. And I remember saying to my staff at one wedding, mid-February, 'This will be our last wedding. So we better make the most of it.' They all looked at me and laughed, as Easter in mid-April was our last wedding for the season. But clearly, She and I were channelling and being told something different.

In a matter of days, my business had gone from a fully booked season of abundance to flatlining in cardiac arrest. Cases started entering our shores. And I remember clearly saying to my husband, 'We need to start thinking about our business, and what that looks like, as spirit, my guidance, is telling me weddings will not be our bread and butter.'

We decided really early to make changes within our business. For ten years I had poured so much love and energy into my business to not let it disappear and fail.

At 11.59 pm on Wednesday 25 March 2020, New Zealand entered a nationwide lockdown.


My first week in lockdown, I was in survival mode. I knew this place and space before I lived there for seven years in my first marriage. I was mentally and physically checking boxes, keeping myself busy, and calling in other realms for help.

By week two, I needed to stop and start having a deeper conversation with self. I remember clearly going to my altar space and locking myself away for hours. I had realised my life was about serving others, but not myself at a soul level, or those around me. There was a lot of shadow stuff that came forward—fears, tears, broken promises, beliefs that I needed to work through—as I was no longer connected to my son, husband or my own self. I was living my life according to what everyone else needed and not what I needed.

I need to stop! And rethink how I was living and showing up in this life. Because to the outside world it looked like I was living my best life, but internally, being in the service of others was suffocating the shit out of me, my marriage and all that I loved.

So I did what I knew would help me. I became still. Still with life.

I lit my altar candle and asked: 'How am I to show up in the world?'

The words were whispered, *As you.*

I had forgotten Who I really was, at a soul level.

Then I felt her presence, and her hug. Anna appeared in my mind's eye, just like we were having a conversation at my breakfast bar over a cuppa.

*Your greatest gift is your ability to see in people's hearts, and help activate healing for others.*

She was right. I knew what she was asking: More from me! And I was scared shitless to my core, goosebumps ran all over my body, and my breath became deeper. I could feel the fear as a teardrop ran across my cheek, and I wiped it away, trying not to cry.

*You can't be scared, as Now is the time, dear friend.*

She was right, I needed to surrender as I needed not only to trust myself, but her love, and our friendship at a deeper level.

So in that moment, as friends do, we made a pact, a pinky swear.

Anna was to find me my people and I would show up and speak my truth no matter what I felt or how uncomfortable I would be.

And so it was.

And so it is.

The more I show up, the more I am rewarded.

The day I signed the publishing contract for this book, I knew it to be true. It was three years since Anna's passing, to the day. And as I pulled up my drive, having dropped my son off at school, she appeared beside me in the car, saying, *No matter how fearful you get, promise me you will keep showing up, and I promise you I will keep leading you.*

For so long I have wanted to be accepted, to be loved, and seen for who I truly am.

Being an awakened soul on this earth is lonely at times.

As I see the looks that are given over teacups across the room, the whispers, judgement, I hear the comments, I know what you're thinking if you acknowledge my post on Facebook, what will that mean? I am the mum standing at the school gate by herself because I see the world differently. And people are afraid to talk to me.

I thought for many years I was broken. I thought I needed to be fixed, to fit into what was the normal part of society.

But what I have learnt is I am not broken.

I am not here to be feared.

I need to honour who I am to heal.

And still, as much as I know I could conform to make those around me comfortable, I decided, *To hell with that. I can't do that anymore.* I am here to take brave actions, to stand in courage, and if I am to be wounded by humanity again and again, it is a choice that I can now live with.

Why?

Because doing the work, the real work in this lifetime means getting closer to your authentic self and truth.

And when I am guided to her, she never leaves me. She fills me.

Have I been sacred? Hell yes! Have I been frightened? Yes! But the more I step forward into my fear of the internal darkness, the more I am led back home to myself, that part I had forgotten, and along the way I have reclaimed particles of my soul that I didn't know were lost

I am still yet to fully understand the unseen knowledge, the higher realms, frequencies and my gift.

I work daily on letting go, being still, surrendering and asking. It's a constant battle, a deeper conversation I have with myself.

Does this make me normal? Who knows?

But it makes me real!

To be true to oneself, without fear, is the greatest gift we can give ourselves.

And only you can honour this.

This is what I know to be true. This is what I no longer can push down, disconnect from, or run from.

As this part of me, she is wise. She lives within, she sometimes shows up outside of me—that voice in my head, that shiver down my spine, that scratch on my head, the goosebumps on my skin, the buzzing in my ear, the energy in my womb space. She speaks before I realise what she is saying. She is a channel, a vessel, for greater healing within me and for those that receive her through my medicine.

She is part of me, as I am part of her.

A woman that truly owns her awakened self and embodies all aspects of self is a woman truly empowered and sovereign, and is a woman feared.

As empowered, sovereign, women create change.

We no longer can be still, we are being asked to act!

My place and space in this world is to show up, and if others feel uncomfortable, that's not mine to own, that's their work.

Every light-bulb moment, breadcrumb or light activation that pushes me forward has come as a summons from her, a reclaiming, remembering a calling.

And for those who think we are broken.

We are not broken.

We need to start remembering and come forward out of the shadows to heal ourselves, and those around us—as we don't need to be fixed, we just need to remember who we are.

And welcome her home x

# About the author

# Larina Tiffen-Fuller

Larina Tiffen-Fuller (aka Lilly) is a Visionary, Priestess, Activator, Author, Medium. She is the Founder and Owner of the award-winning Miss Lilly's Catering and Priestess Lilly. She is a trained counsellor, Beautiful You life coach, spellcaster, manifesting queen, channeller of other divine frequencies and seeker of the unknown. She lives with her husband Kristian, and their son Thomas in Aotearoa, New Zealand, in a countryside town called Rangiora. This is where she feels deeply grounded. She believes in Angels, Goddesses, Light beings, Cosmos energy, and magic. She knew at a very young age she could see, and sense the world differently to other people, and it is from there she will share her story about acceptance of her true self and her gift. She feels now is the time that she can honour her true authentic self and show up in the world as we are being called to co-create a new World.

Connect with Larina to see her offerings, book one on one sessions, listen to her podcast or do an online course. Discount code 10%

off her online courses and school: THISIKNOWTOBETRUE10

Join Awakening SHE facebook community space, where the author does channel messages, live readings and energy forecasts: https://www.facebook.com/groups/676257139403651

**Facebook, Priestess Lilly**
**Instagram @priestesslillyawakening**
**www.priestesslilly.com**

✳

# 10.

# Following true north

## LISA KOTZ

Not all domestic violence survivors are able to tell their stories. Not all women who experience domestic violence survive. Their truths are often lost in the silence and shame that shrouds the painful and horrific reality that in the year 2020, in New South Wales alone, 32,078 domestic violence assaults were reported to police.[1] The reality that in seventy-four per cent of those assaults, the perpetrator is a man, and that over half of those assaults are by an intimate partner or spouse—current or previous. And those numbers are only the cases that are actually reported.

Telling my story now isn't easy, nor convenient. But it is important and it needs to be told. I want to honour my younger self by witnessing her growth and courage.

I was in a relationship with a man, who—over years—mentally, emotionally, psychologically and physically wore me down, hurt me and tried to break me. This story isn't about them. It's about me, for me, for the women of my lineage and every other person who has been harmed and oppressed by patriarchal, hierarchal systems of power, abuse, control, silence and expectations. This is for you too. This is my story of trust, triumph and truth.

---

[1] Source: NSW Bureau of Crime Statistics and Research.

It was early spring in 2012. The season of rebirth and renewal was emerging. The coastal nights were still cool and the days warm, but there was a freshness in the air. It's my second favourite time of the year after my first love, the introverted cocoon of winter.

The weather was at the front of my mind as this spring was set to be one of the most joyous, fun and glamorous times in my life. I was marrying my long-term partner—part of my life plan I had pretty much all mapped out. I'd already smashed through all of my career goals by the age of twenty-eight and had been appointed my dream roles of Clinical Nurse Specialist and Flight Nurse at one of the state's busiest trauma intensive care units. My relationship was next on the list. Marriage seemed like the next right (heteronormative) thing to do! At the time I didn't really see it going any other way. I had a programmed drive to achieve 'success' and abide by social expectations—marriage was the next thing.

The progress I made in my nursing career was a testament to the huge personal growth and development I had worked on since leaving high school and it was something I was truly proud of achieving. Work was my initiation into womanhood as it transformed the shy, quiet girl I was into the assertive, empathetic and capable woman that I am. I was doing life saving, time-critical healthcare in a team of awesome people and it boosted my self-worth immensely.

The work provided me with so much fulfilment and purpose. Being with patients and families on what were often the worst days of their life, offering support, care and skill was and still is the highest privilege I can imagine for myself. I was a highly trained nurse leader, directly impacting people's lives, and I regard the responsibility and magnitude of that so highly and reverently to this day.

For a time I believed I could literally take on anything. I was at the apex of my career and it felt incredible.

I look back now, though, and see I was leading a polar-opposite double life. My life at work—confident, purposeful, engaged. And my life at home—insular, cloistered, miserable.

My early ideas of what a committed, serious relationship looked like and felt like came strongly from my own family. For most of us, as we grow up we form via our closest people our initial ideas of the world and what we should value and how we should behave and respond to each other and to life. I thought every family was like my family. My parents were married in their very early twenties and had me the year after their wedding. My grandparents on both sides were married in their twenties too and remained together into their elder years. Always together, even with the arguments and the dynamics of life. For the longest time, I thought I would have a husband and one day a family of my own. It never occurred to me that I could choose differently.

My childhood memories of mundane weekday evenings would involve Mum working, then coming home to cook the evening meal and prepare the school lunches, and while Dad watched TV after work. At my grandparent's house, Nan always had the dinner table set by 5 pm and food was served at 6 pm, just in time for Pop to come home from work and sit down for a hot meal. The man of the house did some yard work, shed work and basically relaxed after their 'hard day's work' while I watched the women go from task to work to task every single day.

As a girl, my complete vision of being an adult was that I would have a husband and a child by the same age as my parents, I would also go to work, and that would be life! The wife role was modelled so clearly by my mother, my friend's mothers, characters in films and on TV, and my grandmothers, and I took it all to my core. Keep the house running, do the cooking, the cleaning, the grocery shopping, the laundry, the organising ... if you put yourself or your needs first, then you are selfish. If you feel any kind of anger, frustration, sadness or less-than-happy emotion, make sure you express that with some kind of positive twist, or denial, silence, passive aggression or sarcasm, or secret yourself away for a bit and emerge again as if nothing was bothering you. I thought nothing of these behaviours—it just was the way you lived as a woman.

My internal world as a child and adolescent was very deep, imaginative and private. I frequently found myself curiously exploring the world in my own way, often on my own by choice. When I was a teenager I explored the realms of witchcraft and spirituality, where I found so much richness. It sparked my curiosity about the world and how things worked. By my twenties and during this toxic relationship, my spiritual practice was non-existent.

I kept much of my private life exactly that—private from my parents and even some of my friends. It felt safest emotionally to do that, and it served me well (or so I thought), though it also created a large shield of armour around me that I'm still reconfiguring.

My body was, and still is, a highly attuned instrument, sensitive to the emotional energy of others. For the longest time, I didn't realise that most of the anxiety, friction, anger and pain I was feeling probably didn't belong to me. I didn't know what energetic entanglement meant, or what being an empath was, or how to shield but not cut myself off from others. I internalised the feelings I experienced and developed the narrative inside my head that went something like this: *If I behave, be a good girl, stay quiet and not cause problems, then they will be happy and everything will be ok.* In other words, I learnt to 'fawn' and suppress my own needs to appease someone else's state of being. I thought that others' behaviour around and towards me was because of me, therefore I could adapt my behaviour to placate others. To stay safe and invisible. Classic people pleasing.

My report cards all the way through my schooling years always read something like, *Lisa is a quiet and conscientious worker* and *Lisa is caring and considerate*. I learnt very early on that being quiet and diligent while putting others' needs first was valued and rewarded, and therefore was a desirable trait to cultivate and model throughout my life. Straight out of the patriarchy playbook. It really didn't matter how much education I received later in life either. The patriarchal program is invasive and ingrained.

My relationship had been going for eight years. At the time, on some levels, I knew the relationship wasn't healthy. But I convinced myself that we still had so much potential and all it needed was for me to keep trying with it, with him, for him. Even though being in the relationship could be so painful, it was still worth it, I thought. Relationships require sacrifice and putting others before yourself to make it work sometimes, right?

The good times were good. There were some redeeming qualities of the relationship I kept convincing myself were worth it. The nasty moods he would get into, the condescending tones and put-downs that would be launched my way seemed somewhat excusable, tolerable.

I thought I loved him. All that history we had. I thought I could help him. He was just a bit immature, right? He'd been through some stuff, but he kept telling me he was working on it, that he had plans to heal and grow. All he needed was some help and compassion, right? The healer in me thought that was completely reasonable.

What is obvious to me now was nowhere near clear to me then.

The disintegration of my self-worth and self-trust happened slowly over that time, and my purpose warped into managing myself and my life around the destructive behaviour of a grown man.

The manipulation and gradual escalation of the abuse and torment weren't obvious when I was in the thick of it. It was like descending slowly into a fog, and before you know it you're surrounded, you can only see one step in front of you and you have no idea which way to turn next. So you stay put.

I didn't know what narcissistic control and abuse really were until I had extracted myself from them. Even when he tried to strangle me, I found some way to rationalise it away. His erosion of me occurred insidiously, carefully and deliberately.

Looking back, I realised I had experienced daily episodes of gaslighting, emotional manipulation and coercive control. This was well before the pop-psychology infographics that flood social media today and help raise awareness on these issues. I had no idea that what was happening to me was a systematic and classic go-to move of an abuser—one that further disintegrates their victim's sense of self-worth and connection to their strength to increase the abuser's control over them.

I thought I had made my choice of life partner. This was the person I was spending the rest of my life with! Everything else I was putting my mind to, like my career and friendships, was blossoming—why wouldn't my marriage too? I thought I had enough energy, momentum and willpower to pull him up with me. It was going to be great.

I'll never forget the moment though, one afternoon in his company, when a flash of insight arrived like a thunderclap inside my head, many years before the abuse really started. Out of nowhere, demanding attention and unmistakable. A crystal-clear internal voice, my voice, said to me, *This isn't going to last.* A feeling of dread, then panic, then resistance pushed through my body from my head to my toes. I felt my heart contract and stiffen. I pushed my intuition away, denied it completely.

I recall the schism so clearly—that was the exact moment I abandoned myself. Abandoned myself to perform the version of me that I thought I should be, what the patriarchy had trained me to be. I thought I had 'signed the contract', so to speak, and if I went back on my word to him and to myself about my commitment to the relationship, then I would be failing as a woman and as a partner, despite all the evidence that my body and heart were trying to show me. This belief was a trap, and the biggest lie I ever swallowed whole.

For the longest time, I thought I was solely to blame for creating that belief for myself. I had been gaslighting myself! But I know now that I was trying to fit into the predetermined patriarchal gender roles assigned to women that I had seen modelled for me, at any and all cost. To survive, to be seen as successful in life. That belief, combined with my inherent desire to help others and to be the 'good girl' felt like invisible bonds that kept me trapped. Not to mention, my programming as a nurse contributed to this desire to help him and stay the course no matter how bad it got. After all, my profession evolved out of traditional gender roles with women as the caregiver, selfless and subservient—that in many ways in my opinion nursing is still tied in unconscious patriarchal undertones. Needless to say, I've had a lot of unpacking and healing to do.

*\*\*\**

'Oh gosh, congratulations! Can I see a photo of your dress?' The tearoom chatter at work was abuzz, and I reluctantly pulled my phone out of my pocket to show my colleague the posed picture of me under a tree at my own wedding, just three weeks prior. 'Oh wow, you are SO beautiful!' they showered over me.

Inside I was numb. Dissociated. 'Thank you,' I managed, with a half smile. The happiness was feigned. The wedding had happened. So did the last assault, the subsequent arrest, the apprehended violence order and the separation. All in the space of two weeks.

The facade was still up, I didn't know how to proceed really. I was in shock and not fully able to reconcile what had just happened to me, though I was back at work in the hospital and trying to convince myself I was ok. The only people who knew what had happened were my family and my best friend. How the fuck was I supposed to explain all of this? Why was I feeling this intense shame and contraction when I had been assaulted? Harmed, traumatised, violated and reduced to a small quivering shell.

How did I break free? It wasn't anyone else who 'rescued' me. For me, it had to get to the lowest of lows for me to crack open and fully see the bondage I was in and then blindly and completely trust the way out.

Liberation came in another thunderclap of clarity, directly from the purest source of love and support in a moment of extreme fear and duress. To this day I have no other explanation for what transpired on the day, other than it was a mystical experience.

The clearest direction I have ever received in my life came through in stereo to my inner hearing and knowing, gently and firmly, and said, *This ends today.* In that instant, I believed it to be true with the entirety of my being and I surrendered to a level I hadn't known existed until then. I felt held and carried by the most exquisite benevolence and instantaneously I knew that no matter what happened to me, the schism was now healed because I had said yes to myself in a deep and real way, finally.

With those words—and it still moves me to tears of deep gratitude as I write—the patriarchal spell over me was broken and I felt the reverberation through my lineage, through timelines and realities. I knew it was a death and rebirth of me at that exact moment. Everything changed. Every single thing in my life shifted from that day on, for the absolute better. As soon as I could, I called a domestic violence helpline and from there my liberation was set in motion.

And so I continue on the journey of the evolution of myself. Step by step cultivating my sense of self, my sovereignty and agency as a human, and getting to know who I actually am and wish to be outside of the identity of wife, daughter, woman, nurse or any other label I have collected. I'd love to say it's been fantastic and straightforward, but that would be a lie! It's certainly a non-linear experience.

I want to acknowledge, thank and celebrate younger me for her courage and faith despite her fear, pain and uncertainty. She welcomed the next iteration of me in that pivotal moment and I'm really proud of how far I have come, and where I am headed. She put the first crack in many outdated patterns I had been holding on to. She laid the first paver down on my path to becoming a coach and mentor for other women who are reclaiming their self-sovereignty too.

Reflecting on and sharing this is still quite overwhelming at times. The importance of sharing and being witnessed by the community is something that has been intrinsic to my healing and sense of purpose and belonging. It was the cloak of silence that paralysed me and stopped me from reaching out and asking for help, due to the shame and perceived judgement.

The patriarchal framework that demanded the facade of perfection, happiness, control, orderliness and having my shit together—along with not properly acknowledging the serious red flags—certainly contributed to me staying longer in that relationship than was healthy.

What I know to be true, is that even the slightest of realignments back to your true north, guided by your intuition, will steer you in the right direction. It can have the most profound and positive impact on the trajectory of your life even when everything and everyone around you (even your own head) is telling you to conform, submit, hand over your power and obey. The key is to trust and believe in that teeny tiny piece of your true self that you might only have known a mere slice of. It might be your heart, a whisper of self-compassion, or your gut feeling. I know it is so challenging to hear and believe what your inner voice is trying to tell you when there are layers upon layers of social conditioning covering you from it. It is confusing to even know who you actually are and what you really want. The patriarchal structures and the confinement of traditional gender roles will show you the narrow scope that your life decisions should be made within and if those choices are not truly your own, they will never feel expansive, light, or liberating. It's even more of a mind fuck when you realise you have been gaslighting yourself with the internalised misogyny you learnt somewhere along the way. Remember, your truest self only wants the absolute best for you. The highest, brightest and best.

By sharing our stories and witnessing each other, we are slowly but surely unbinding ourselves from silence, shame and isolation and offering balm through support and collective healing. We see ourselves in each other's stories and we reflect each other's humanity and beauty.

I send love to the women of my lineage backwards and forwards in time. I know that every piece of my healing is their healing. It is your healing too.

# About the author

# Lisa Kotz

Lisa Kotz (she/her) is a life and self-sovereignty coach for nurses and healers. Lisa's work during this time of shift and evolution is to support the rise of self-sovereign women who are claiming their personal power and are leading themselves and their communities to experience fuller, richer and authentic connections using innate wisdom, grounded action and deep integrity. She founded her coaching practice Inside The Prism with this vision at the core.

Having been a nurse and healer herself for over twenty years Lisa has supported, guided and professionally cared for others in times of deep personal change, uncertainty and often struggle. As an intensive care nurse she has witnessed the depth and breadth of what people can endure and also triumph over – not just physically but emotionally and spiritually too. Lisa considers this to be the highest honour to walk beside others doing deep inner work and she is passionate about embodying compassion, empathy and love while honouring and promoting personal sovereignty and autonomy.

Through her own experience as a domestic violence survivor Lisa believes the key to self-sovereignty, healing and growth starts with reconnecting with our body and heart and learning to trust your innate wisdom to lead your life with courage and discernment. Lisa has a special gift of holding deep sacred space to support multidimensional healing, learning, transformation and evolution in her private coaching sessions.

Lisa lives on Wonnarua Country on the east coast of Australia with her sweet old mini poodle, surrounded by her life partner, her favourite people and a healthy collection of books on spirituality, stories, magick, mysticism, art, fashion, feminism and growing orchids.

**Website: www.insidetheprism.com**
**Podcast: Spiritually Sovereign**
**https://www.buzzsprout.com/1724785**
**Instagram: www.instagram.com/lisackotz**

# 11.

# Divine leader of change, a woman's rite in a new era of change

## MAREE EDDINGS

I have always known that my being is not for me. That my very existence is owed to someone else, to something else. A promise, if you will, that my birth was about me serving a system first and me as a person second, or even third.

I knew this in my bones and it scared me.

While I never had language for it, I did have the feeling of it. What I didn't know then, but grew to understand, is that I am an energy-sensitive empath and my experience of my life is to experience the feelings of the world around me.

This is how I knew that the system I was born into was bigger than me and it existed in every single person I was surrounded by. The majority of the feelings I experienced were sorrow, pain, frustration and fear. Even in the moments of laughter and fun, there was always the undertone of survival and pain. This did not feel like a safe space for my heart or my dreams.

I remember the day that my feelings were confirmed. As an eight-year-old sitting with my back against the archway between the dining and lounge rooms, I was listening to my mum on the phone. She couldn't see me and we had just gotten a second phone plug and the phone now had a long cord. It was a big upgrade in our house and created greater privacy for phone calls, unless you were sitting where I was.

I was so drawn to this call not because of what was being discussed, but the feeling of my mum's energy. It was so joyous and light. I was fixated, basking in this amazing light that she was emitting. It felt amazing. I felt nourished and my nervous system was relaxed. This did not happen very often. She often felt more worried and fearful. She had reason. So, when this moment of peace and lightness was here, it was not to be missed.

So there I was, sitting in a way that I would not be caught, basking in that big light. I was not aware of much that was being said, it was all about how she felt.

Then I heard my name. My mum was talking to her mum about the day she and her friends had had. A girl's day where they went to see a psychic and had lunch, and from what I could tell, had a great time. As soon as I heard my name, I was snapped out of the trance I was in and quickly became attuned to the conversation.

It went something like this: 'Oh, and Maree, yes she is going to be fine. She is going to be married young and she will have twins. She is going to be taken care of. It will all be great. She will be very happy.'

As I listened, I felt the blood drain from my face and my stomach start to churn. I loved that she felt so happy, but I knew that I was not going to do any of that. That is not what I am here to do and I think it is going to break my mum's heart.

Her light was so big, I didn't want that feeling to ever end. I didn't want to cause her pain. I wonder if she knew what her light felt like.

I felt paralysed. The sensation was so strong and I felt bad. While I didn't have language for what was happening, I felt like I had been split down the middle knowing that there was this plan for me, being a girl and all—expectations that this bigger system had for me that I didn't want anything to do with.

So, I became two people. One that stayed under the radar enough to appease the world around me. You know, the good girl, people pleaser, that kind of stuff. I focused on achieving because that seemed to make everyone happy and I wasn't going to cause them any pain. My other side didn't completely leave me. She had this kicker of an attitude that was never that far under the surface. She had passion but she never really spoke about what was in her heart or what her soul felt like. However, at times she would spark debate and challenge. She enjoys that a lot.

It felt like I was walking a tightrope. Everything looked like it should from the outside but never felt right on the inside.

So, I just got better at achieving and, in turn, denying. At times this wrestle brought me to my knees with feelings of depression and anxiety. At other times it fuelled me to make a change in the world and I would stand up and fight, but it was never with my whole heart or with my soul. It felt like a long winding road. With each turn off my path feeling like I was being poked in my solar plexus and of course it was asking me to make it stop, but I kept going pain and all.

It would take about thirty years for the full force of my eight-year-old self's knowledge and heart to resurface, and once that genie was out of the bottle, she was never going back in.

After building a 'successful' career and working myself to what I can only describe as breaking point physically, emotionally and spiritually, I had to make a change. I had to admit to myself that I could no longer ignore this other part of me. The part that was intuitive, energetically sensitive and connected. This was that part that was demanding I feed it, and it was not going to take no for an answer.

It would be lovely to say that this is the end of the story, with a nice, tight Tiffany bow perfectly tied around my life. This was only the beginning.

Once I extracted myself from my career, the real insights and education began. The first tidal wave was the realisation that I had been upholding the very system I knew needed to change. That regardless of all my hard work and talent the fight and the work that I had put in, nothing had really changed. Not a single thing.

The world was still dominated by white men, celebrated for their hierarchy of thinking, was very much entrenched, and people were still experiencing BS leadership in business and in life. While I was in the room, I might have been having an impact, like many others; but as soon as we left the room the system took hold again.

My heart broke with the realisation that I had internalised the system so much, I was part of it. I had held this belief that because I was not really part of it, I was, well, not really part of it. I was wrong. My internalisation of the misogyny of the system didn't change it. It just changed me. It took me further away from my deep knowing and wisdom of who I was.

I was pissed. I cried for weeks. I felt ashamed. I was embarrassed. Once all of that stopped, I got angry.

I was glad that for the first time in my life, my anger had a purpose and a reason. I was no longer going to apologise for this, not like my good girl had been doing. Stuffing down her feelings until she made herself sick.

The impact this had meant I started to ask questions. Questions that I had stopped asking. My mum used to say I asked so many questions about everything and it drove her nuts. This was something I had stopped doing. It was something I needed to keep doing.

This was the main question that I kept hearing: If the system of patriarchy is so bad, and has no redeeming features, then why is it still so embedded in our culture and society?

It seemed like a question that was too big for me. It lit a fire in my belly to find out more and to find out why. I have been growing into this question ever since.

This is what I know.

The system that we live by didn't just turn up one day. There wasn't a meeting nor memo sent out, nor cupcakes with a relevant logo, nor a reveal party to celebrate the occasion. There were no meeting notes that said *Ok, from now on, this is how things are going to be and everyone will comply.* It took time and it was based on a changing belief system. One that was born from fear and scarcity. It started with a focus on women and stripping them of what was considered their power. It used violence and murder to embed the culture and used division and separation to do its bidding.

It created an all-or-nothing thought process and taught people to think in terms of a hierarchy. It has a narrow band of thought and it is obsessed with power over others. It uses comparison to keep the masses in line and when it needed a bigger push for power, it created this thing called race.

It has been successful in turning humans against humans by convincing them to vacate their own humanity. The narrow thinking means that it only accesses a fraction of what can be possible, and it recycles these behaviours over and over again.

This type of thinking does not exist by itself. It dances with a level of consciousness. This is the core reason the system has stayed in control for so long.

The system of patriarchy was born through the behaviours of the contracted masculine energy. This is why we feel it. It has a dance partner in the contracted feminine. Together they can shimmy up and down and back and forth, giving you a sense of freedom and control. They can feel lighter than they did a few years ago and you may even feel like you are dancing a whole new dance. However, while they are in play—with their denying, justifying, blaming, all-or-nothing, judgement, comparison, victimhood, martyrdom dance steps—you are still upholding the system they created.

You and I live with them every day. With our doubts and fears, judgements of ourselves and others, the need to compare and react with the energy of a victim just so we remember we are alive and that we haven't been swallowed whole.

Yes, you may have stretched your consciousness out of the deep, entrenched behaviours, but until we release the system fully and adopt a new consciousness, then we are always PINKING up the PATRIARCHY. Trying to soften its blow and create redemption where there is none.

Until now.

Each generation of women that has come before us has played a role. Each woman today plays a role. Each phase of our life has a purpose and a season. Women who are what we refer to as Generation X (and I include those who like to be called Xennials) have entered the phase of their life where the role they are asked to play cannot be denied.

As women who have experienced the most change of any generation, we were the first to access higher education as a collective and enjoy the work of the women that came before us, We have built careers and our own businesses which has given us access to money and new life experiences. We have been in this game of change since the beginning of our birth and we understand what it takes to navigate it successfully,

We are also in the time of our life where we have no fucks left to give. Not because we are vengeful or full of spite but because we have arrived at the place we are meant to be. Accessing our full power. Wanting more out of our life and the lives of those we love.

The combination is more powerful than the experience of any generation of women before. Of course, we will not and cannot do this alone. The paths our mothers and grandmothers walked and the path that our daughters and nieces are imagining are all part of the change.

None of us is better or worse than the other. However, we do all have a part to play. Individually and as a collective.

This is our rite of passage. To reclaim ourselves from the system that has tried its hardest to rid itself of us.

A reclaiming of the patriarchal story that has separated and had us competing is a place to start. The energy of this generation is palpable. We are not here to be separated.

There are too many of us now asking these questions. Too many of us want to expand our thinking and live outside of this hideous system.

We are rewriting what power and influence mean. There are too many of us reclaiming our own power and stepping away.

What do we do next?

How do we build this so that we can lead our way out?

Is it really possible to dismantle this world that has conditioned us all so well?

I say yes. Here is why.

The dance that the patriarchal system moves to is finite and constrained. It relies on specific behaviours being in play, and without them, it ceases to exist.

I know—can it be that simple? Well, if you stop behaving in the image of the system, what is left?

As Einstein (or his wife, depending on what you have read) said: 'No problem can be solved from the same level of consciousness that created it.'

Patriarchy is a problem to be solved.

As Andre Lorde puts it: 'The master's tools will never dismantle the master's house.'

So, the hierarchy must go.

When we remember that the system has a feeling based on a vibration of energy, then we know it's consciousness. Every time. So yes, it can be changed.

If we want to lead the way out of this system and adopt a new way, to really be the Divine Leaders of Change, then our role is to commit to a change in consciousness until we are out of the system for good.

This is something my eight-year-old has always known; even when she didn't have language for it, she had a knowledge. She knew she didn't have all the resources and neither did the people around her. She does now and so do you.

Shifting our energy consciousness is a new dance. A new way that our internal energies of masculine and feminine dance together. It is a full, infinite space built on trust and transparency, wisdom and compassion, and discernment of energy. There is no need for a hierarchy to keep people small or for power to be about anyone but you. A place where humanity and a strong economy are not seen as mutually exclusive.

Yes, this is what I know for sure, and I know that every other person who is here to lead change and understands energy knows too.

The energy that you feel is not lying, it never was. It is the most powerful, reliable and consistent form of data you have access to. As an energetic being, you are felt before you are known, and your energy consciousness is the impact of your behaviour. Yes, it can be seen and it can be felt.

The way out is via energy consciousness.

Our energy consciousness informs us clearly of where we are in the system. We don't have better energy or better consciousness. We can only have more expanded spaces or less expanded spaces. The patriarchy is a contracted space. So, when we feel like we are in a higher level of consciousness but are still applying a hierarchy in our thoughts and decision making, we have stretched the contraction, but not released it.

Expanded energy consciousness has no conditions. It has limitless potential. It relies on us to embody and take our hand off the support structure that the patriarchy's hierarchy provides. It is full of safety and trust.

So, no matter how much you have stretched your consciousness, until we let go, we will always be in that shimmy dance the patriarchy provides us.

We see this most clearly in our relationships with other people. Regardless of what title you give yourself or the relationship, the experience of this hierarchy is palpable in every person we are connected with. It is even with people we don't know and will never meet.

Our ability to feel safe in the presence of others has everything to do with our level of consciousness and relationship with energy. The more we lean out of the conditions and the structures and lean towards joy, compassion, transparency and discernment of energy, the boxes fall away. The layers disappear and the energy, well, that is divine.

Why should we want any of that?

For any of us to be able to lead change, like, life-transforming change, we first must be able to hold and embody the consciousness of where we want to go. Not have the answers or the solutions, that is ego talk. This is how we truly bring people together to collaborate and remove constricted and narrow decision making, so that we stop the continually cycling and gaslighting structure and start to experience true connection.

This is the role of the Divine Leader. To let go of pushing their competency to the front and learn how to lead with a healer's heart. To hold space for other human beings and see them and hear them.

I know that you already see the BS in the hierarchy. It is so much easier to spot these days. That means you have changed, it has not.

What does this feel like? I am talking about energy, after all. It is all about the connection to the feeling.

Leaders who embrace their Divine Leadership feel grounded, clear, concise and safe. They open spaces for people to explore, even in a basic conversation. There is no performance or seeking of validation. They leave this feeling of transparency and you start to melt the walls of complexity.

Imagine if that was the kind of energy you were around more. Or if you were even the one leading that dance.

This is what the divine masculine and feminine feel like when they dance together.

Joyous.

I know you have felt this. Perhaps it has been in moments with other women or relationships. It fills you up and the peace and connection are undeniable. You may hold it for moments, days or even months. When we turn our attention to this place and want it to be the predominant feeling and focus, then we are dissolving everything that is not it.

I know this can be easier said than done. The familiarity with the old system provides comfort even when it is abhorrent.

I often ask why we might fear this space of expansion. Is it because we don't feel that it is possible? Are we scared that our heart may actually burst open with all the joy? I think it is only because we haven't realised yet that we are not doing this alone, so we haven't fully let go. Imagine what will happen when we do realise that our hearts together will not shatter but only expand more.

For me, I have craved that feeling in my life and especially in relationships with others. I have found it every now and then. It has scared me if I am honest, and I am now getting much better at it because I seek it.

My mum had that energy, maybe yours does or did too. I have known that feeling since I was young and I think this is why I have kept searching for it. How could I not?

The joyous feeling of my mum's energy wasn't something that I felt often, but I yearned for it. It was so big so bright and full of such love. Her middle name was Joy after all. When it came, it was like this ocean of full-body-shaking laughter and it was infectious. She was however living her life, caught up in her beliefs, fears and experiences; she was conditioned, after all, to the same system as I was, so at times it was challenging to feel.

When it came back, however, it was with full force.

She got sick and it happened quickly. In the last months of her life, I was so honoured to care for her. As challenging as it was, I wouldn't change it for anything. I got to experience and feel her light and power once more, at times feeling like that eight-year-old basking in her light all over again. She was unfettered and raw. She was shining with all her heart, laughter, cheekiness and might.

We shared moments I would never have had if I weren't there. At night we would chat. Sometimes it was silly talk that had us giggling and laughing hard, and other times it was filled with long pauses. Neither of us really wanted to acknowledge what was actually going on.

In what would be one of our last chats while she was at home, she said this to me. 'I have been waiting. Waiting for people to grow up, for them to stop using me, for them to stop using emotional blackmail, for them to see me and respect me. I have never been able to say no, even when I tried it was like it made it all worse. So, I kept waiting. Thinking that if I was good enough, they would stop. But they never did.'

This was not said in regret; it was more of a realisation and reflection, as she knew she was entering the final days of her life here on Earth. We both knew what and who she was talking about. Like a collection of memories all rolled into one. All with her left waiting.

If I can leave you with anything about what I know to be true about being a leader as a woman who wants to bring change to this world, it's please stop waiting.

The system will not change or stop itself.

That is for us to do.

# About the author

# Maree Eddings

Maree is an Energy Sensitive, Change Leader and Energy Healer who is on a mission to expand the energy consciousness of the world through her training programs Divine Leaders of Change Sistermind and The Energy Academy.

She is the host of the podcast Divine Leaders of Change and her aim is for us to ask and ponder the following three questions:

What if you were never conditioned with a Patriarchal mindset, structure or system?

Who would you be instead?

And now that we are here how do we lead our way out of it?

This is her ride or die focus for how she wants to contribute to the world and help woman expand their energy consciousness so that they too can hold their power in any situation and in any room and as a result shift that paradigm that we all experience.

It is time for women to step into their role as a Divine Leader with curiosity and a knowing that this is the role they were born to play.

**www.mareeeddings.com**

# 12.

# Intuitively grow your fearless flow

## VANESSA NOVISSIMO WRIGHT

'What if everything you've been conditioned to deny about yourself was actually your gift?'

These words crash over me. I am sitting cross-legged in a corner of my bedroom. When I come back up for air, I am in tears.

Tears of joy.

Tears of gratitude.

Tears of acceptance.

Sarah, a friend and an energy healer, is on the other end of the phone and we're in the middle of an intense session. I'm also in the middle of an intense season of my life as I ponder Sarah's magical words.

What if?

What if I've been denying my gift?

### Overwhelmed with overwhelm

I am rifling through old photos when I find one from eleven years ago. I have very few photos of me and my children from this period of our lives. In the photo, I am sitting on the couch with a half smile, my hair is dishevelled and I have that tired-mummy look in my dark brown eyes. On my lap are the two-year-old twins, grumpy from too-short naps. My energetic four-year-old is hamming it up for the camera, as usual.

I'm overwhelmed with joy. Conceiving, carrying and birthing these babies in a very short period of time was a miracle. And I know this.

But I was also just flat-out overwhelmed.

My health was all over the map. I was losing weight, and also dealing with a multitude of issues that conventional doctors could not seem to piece together or help me understand. I experienced frequent fainting episodes. I was knee-deep in nutrition research, parenting research and women's health research. I was also knee-deep in diapers, snack time, craft time, playtime and bedtime. This was my daily routine. Rinse and repeat.

I'm tried to do all the 'right' things. This was my default mode. I was a rules follower. I was a people pleaser. I was a helper. Sometimes I did things well and other times, I am way off base. So, I kept pushing forward. I kept that deep sense of joy tucked down so I could keep going.

This photo feels like yesterday but also a lifetime ago. I am that woman in the photo, yes, but I've healed in so many ways. I'm still learning and growing. And, of course, I still get tired.

This is why I write.

This is why I show up.

This is why I want to connect and encourage others.

This is why I FLOW.

## Finding FLOW

Flow—the action of moving along in a steady, continuous stream. Think of all the things that flow, like water, electricity, ideas and creativity. When things flow there is movement and purpose—no stagnation and no blockages.

The concept of flow came into my life several years ago. I was working with a wonderful coach and she asked if I was in my flow. Truthfully, I was feeling stuck in many areas of my life. I was in my early forties and juggling homeschooling, working from home and health issues (me and two of my children), and I was feeling disconnected from my passions and purpose.

So, no, I was definitely *not* going with my flow.

A few days after our session, her words still lingered. What would it be like to be in my flow? What did that even mean?

As a writer, I love acronyms, so I started playing around with the letters F, L, O and W. After a few iterations and with a desperate need to acknowledge my own needs, dreams and desires, I created my concept of FLOW:

> *Feed your body in a way that honours your unique self*
> *Love yourself and lean into your season of life*
> *Own your time and space*
> *Weed out what's not working and welcome something new*

It was time to show up in my life as a stronger and more connected woman.

When I shared my concept of FLOW, I was pleased with how it resonated with people in real life and in the online community. Raising a family or caring for others *and* taking good care of yourself are not mutually exclusive. I've been there, friends. I've been the excited new homeschooling mama who researches everything and throws herself in headfirst. I've been the woman whose body shut down multiple times because I ignored the warning signs. I've been the mother juggling children with major health issues, moving and job changes.

Just like so many of you.

Taking care of YOU isn't selfish. Your mental, physical, emotional and spiritual health are not secondary to washing the dishes, preparing meals, reading and responding to all the work emails, helping your child with homework, or tending to all the tasks we manage each day. They are the *most* important. Period.

### Intuitively grow your fearless FLOW

Do you know what you truly need? Do you want to be in your own flow? You have a voice inside of you—it's your intuition. And it can be trusted and grow over time.

When you're in your fearless flow, you're open to new things and cultivating a life you love. When you connect intuition and fearless flow, you show up each day as your perfectly imperfect authentic self.

Let's dive in …

### Feed your body in a way that honours your unique self

What's your relationship like with food and feeding yourself? Is food a pain point? A struggle or a constant battle? Do you want to feel vibrant and connected in your body but you're not sure what that looks like for you?

I've tried nearly every diet on the planet—you can take a look at my cookbook selection for yourself. I've been on a health and wellness journey for two decades. I've immersed myself in nutrition books, blogs, seminars, courses, coaching, podcasts and more. From balancing my hormones to losing weight and figuring out gut health—I've tried almost everything.

And you know what? I'd feel better for a short period of time, or until I got bored. I struggled to find *something*—a plan, a diet, etc.—that I could consistently do each day without making myself exhausted or creating an unhealthy relationship with food.

After some serious reflection and support from two amazing coaches, I asked myself what it would be like to feed my body in a way that honours my unique self.

Yes, it took me a long time to arrive here. And while I'm grateful for all the knowledge I've gained the last twenty years and how I've helped my family's health, it was time to truly get back to basics.

For me, it means going back to a Mediterranean way of eating, as I am one-hundred per cent Italian. It means looking back at old family recipes and learning more about ancestral foods so that I can move forward each day feeling grounded and nourished. It means asking my body what *she* wants before each meal. It means eating high-quality dark chocolate *every single day*. It means not berating myself for food choices.

If this sounds challenging, it is! I have worked with coaches who specialise in this area, and it really helped. Research intuitive eating. Get back in touch with your family's roots and recipes. Write down a list of foods that make you feel good! Grab some new cookbooks or visit some new food blogs. Invent a few recipes for yourself. Try some different fruits and veggies the next time you go grocery shopping.

When you start feeding yourself well, your energy levels will increase and you'll enjoy food more. You can honour yourself in the most beautiful way.

### Love yourself and lean into your season of life

Our lives, like the seasons, shift and flow. How can you love yourself and lean into your current season of life?

All of us are in different seasons of life—what's working for you or causing struggles is different from your friend, your co-worker, and me. Maybe your days feel like a blur or maybe you're in a state of transition and nothing feels settled. Maybe you're in a particularly challenging season of life and you feel like you've lost yourself and you. are. drained.

Feeling drained can feel like so many different things. The worst is when you feel drained and then feel bad about feeling drained (as though you shouldn't feel drained) so you pretend you're not drained and then, well, you know … you're drained.

May I share some encouraging words? When you constantly wish for things to be different or for your life to feel like it's finally 'together', or you're living in the past or pining for the future, you might be making yourself feel more miserable. You miss out on the goodness of the present and all this particular season of life can offer—yes, even with all of its challenges.

Loving yourself right now, as you are, doesn't have to be complicated, but it does take being intentional. Start by finding one small thing each day that nourishes your mind, body and soul. Write yourself a list, schedule it into your planner, or set reminders on your phone.

Need some ideas? I've got you covered:

- Take a walk outside alone and listen to your favourite music or podcast
- Call a friend and talk and laugh and cry
- Read a book that delights you or transports you
- Eat something delicious that is just for you
- Write in your journal or draw or sketch or paint

- Knit or cross-stitch
- Practise yoga or meditate
- Buy yourself flowers

I have experienced dark seasons of life. I have been on the bathroom floor crying and I've walked out of my house to catch my breath, and I've driven around in my car blasting music so I could come back to myself. I have wondered if life would ever feel 'normal' again. Self-care is not something that should be reserved for when you're already burned out. No, it must be something you actively make space for every day—no matter what season of your life you're in. Take two minutes, ten minutes, thirty minutes, an entire day! Love yourself right now in this moment and lean into your life.

**Own your time and space**

Here's my truth: Owning my time and space is the most challenging part of finding my flow. These are two areas that I've struggled with most of my life—but especially since becoming a mother sixteen years ago. I then added homeschooling and also working from home. And that is precisely why I *had* to include them when I created this plan.

Being in my flow is also about growth and doing what I can to be intentional. It's about swimming through the various currents—sometimes it feels easy and refreshing and other times not so much. It all counts. And it comes down to this: I'm here for connection. It's what brings me joy. Owning my time and space equals connection.

How are you spending your time and how's your physical space? Are you collapsing into bed at the end of each day? Do you feel like you're always playing catch up or always 'behind' some arbitrary schedules? Do you bring beauty into your home? Do you have a special space in your home that is just for you?

First, let's talk about time. Not owning my time and telling myself that I didn't need rhythms or routines or structure actually created a ton of stress, for me and my family.

Owning your time can be done and it can be freeing. It takes some planning. It takes asking for help. It takes sharing with your family or friends or community what you are saying NO to and what you are saying YES to in the particular season you're in right now. It might take re-examining your beliefs around structured time and routines and what serves you best in your current season of life.

Now for owning your space …

I was the mum who let everything go and moved from day to day with whatever messes were around until eventually I got so frustrated that I turned into a cleaning machine. I implemented regimented cleaning schedules and systems in order to keep our house looking like we didn't even live in it at all.

I finally found a happy medium where I brought the family on board to help with daily contributions. I've let things go (like the constant nagging for kids to clean their rooms), and I've taken it upon myself to create soothing and functional spaces in our home.

The best thing I did was create something I call my *self-care station*. I need my things to be out and visible or else I forget about them over the course of the day or week or month.

My station is sacred and visually appealing to me. My station has vitamins, essential oils, books, beautiful art, poetry and a candle.

Your station can have all the items you need to stay in your flow. Decorate it with special photos, flowers, essential oils, crystals, etc. It could be an area in your kitchen or a desk, a bedside table, or even a simple shelf! You get to have fun, take a deep breath, and create a small space of beauty. For you. Just you. It's one simple way you can own your space and keep yourself connected to what truly matters.

**Weed out what's not working and welcome something new**
It can be difficult to hear our soul whispering to us. It's simple to push these soul whispers to the side, to bury them in a box marked *Come back to later* and then forget them, or worse, ignore these whispers altogether.

I get it. We are living life. And life is messy and loud and painful and joyful and changes on a dime. Roads get blocked and paths change. People come and go. Heartaches and heartbreaks.

What needs to be weeded out so that you can clearly hear your soul whispers? Once you weed out what's not working, what can you welcome with joy and curiosity?

Start by putting everything on the table: activities, meal plans (or lack of them), chores, jobs, classes, holidays—anything goes! You can work your schedule to best serve your needs (remember you're *owning your time* now). This might be hard for you and your family— especially if you're used to doing *all the things*. Start pruning. Get some white space and breathing room for the things that *do* matter and the things that *do* bring joy. It will bring a sense of relief and potentially open the door to new opportunities.

What is one thing you've wanted to start doing? Name it and then find a way to add it into your life. For me, it's been daily mindful movement and starting a life coach certification program. I had to step away from some other opportunities in my life to make this work and also had to get the family on board. And while this period of transition is challenging, it's absolutely worth it.

Soul whispers flow around you, encircling you with warmth and creativity and purpose and authenticity. Now is the time to connect with them.

**Embracing your daily FLOW**

Once I began my own healing process (energy work, coaching, therapy, journaling, reading and self-study), I began to step out with more confidence and share my imperfect story. I've experienced deep heartache, health issues, postpartum depression, and more. And here I am. I am continually learning, growing and flowing. Sharing this concept of FLOW with others has become my passion and purpose.

Take time to honour the flow day to day, month to month and season to season. Be mindful of how you feel, look for intentional connections, and remember to revise routines and rhythms. Step into a new season of FLOW with eyes and heart and hands wide open.

The beautiful thing about finding your flow is that it evolves over time. It is not stagnant. It is not rigid. We must feed our unique selves, lean in and love ourselves, own our time and space, and weed out what's not serving us.

I would like to leave you with this poem. My hope is that it will ignite you to intuitively grow your fearless flow.

*This is listening*
*This is speaking up*
*This is questioning*
*This is standing in my truth*
*This is setting boundaries*
*This is laughing*
*This is crying*

*This is learning*

*This is embracing my body*

*This is listening to my intuition*

*This is lip gloss and eye cream*

*This is a sacred journey*

*This is creating*

*This is poetry*

*This is singing off key*

*This is softening*

*This is praying*

*This is movement*

*This is calling on my ancestors*

*This is loss*

*This is joy*


*This is encouragement*

*This is light*

*This is faith*

*This is purpose*

*This is connection*

*This is finding my flow*

**This I know is true**

# About the author

# Vanessa Novissimo Wright

Vanessa Wright is a writer and coach who works with mothers of pre-teens and teens intuitively grow their fearless flow by uncovering their passions and purpose. She helps them create sustainable self-care practices so they can connect create, and come back to themselves.

She is a Beautiful You Coaching Academy life coach and also works for a popular children's growth mindset company as the homeschool liaison and Facebook manager. She has been a contributing writer to the The Homeschool Mom blog and helped launch the Carolina Homeschool Conference in 2019. She also enjoys chatting on podcasts about motherhood, homeschooling, and self-care.

Prior to raising her family and homeschooling, Vanessa worked in marketing communications and public relations. She holds a Bachelor of Arts in Professional Writing and French from Carnegie Mellon University in Pittsburgh, Pennsylvania, USA.

Vanessa is a long-time homeschooling mom to three teens. She loves books, journals, hot tea, and high-quality dark chocolate. She and her family live in Raleigh, North Carolina in the United States.

**Instagram @vanessanwright**
**www.vanessanwright.com**

# 13.

# Inner narrative

## THEANA JORDANN

I remember that day like it was yesterday, the words *You are not good enough* plastered in my mind like a repetitive light signal that would never shut off. Each time I stepped in front of the mirror, the words would get brighter and louder, forcing me to a standstill, making it impossible to escape from.

My perception of myself was so flawed that all I saw was a girl who was wrapped up in her own shame, guilt and insecurities. It got to a point where I was being weighed down by others' opinions and strangled by words that would later haunt me for a good portion of my life. Putting me in a place of exhaustion as I was always trying to live up to expectations that I knew I was never going to fulfil.

It wasn't until I came to my breaking point that I realised I was never going to achieve the standard of beauty that I so desperately craved. I had been going around in circles fighting for my truth, fighting for my identity but in the end all I was left with were the pieces of me that I was trying to erase.

After that self-realisation, the answers started boiling up to the surface, causing every cell in my body to feel uneasy and exposed. With every mistake, failure and regret, my body would tremble with fear, as I was never able to admit what my soul was trying to tell me for all these years.

At this point in my life, I knew I couldn't keep going the way I was going. Everything that I did felt forced, and everything that followed felt broken. I didn't love my life, and more importantly I didn't love myself. How was I supposed to embody self-love when I didn't even know who I was? How was I supposed to love my soul, when most of my life we had been strangers who just inhabited the same body?

At just sixteen months, I was adopted and brought to Canada to start a whole new life, with a whole new family. I am very grateful for everything my family has done for me, but if I am being honest, it wasn't always sunshine and rainbows. Being surrounded by a family who didn't look like me left me with a lot of questions and uncertainty that I couldn't let go of. The gap that I created between me and them became so instrumental that I felt like I was always on the outside looking in. Unfortunately, that led me to not celebrate my difference, but become ashamed of it. This wasn't instilled in me from a young age, but bit by bit, parts of me were floating away the more I let the narrative play that I wasn't good enough.

Furthermore, growing up I was surrounded by a sea of white. I was the literal black sheep in every outing, every activity, in most communities, and even in my own home. With that came the feeling of immense pressure, but more importantly I slowly started to lose control of the chatter that was going on in my own mind. Of course, for the most part I was always included, but I always knew that my skin would be a problem for some people. The glances and stares, even at a young age I knew what they meant. The incessant need to touch my hair like I was an animal at the zoo became an unwanted but predictable act that I assumed I had to accept.

Deep down I knew I belonged too, but I slowly started to lose the war within myself and I became my own worst enemy. I was no longer embracing my truth but running away from it.

When I reached a certain age, appearance became everything to me, and this is where my strength was truly tested. Most people that I saw on my TV didn't look like me, and I knew I wasn't the 'standard of beauty' that others admired or looked up to (even my own Barbies would torture me). But what became my main focus was my hair, and it was the battle that started before I even knew it had begun.

At a young age, the term 'difficult' was used to describe my natural hair. It was unmanageable, unkempt and something that needed to be dealt with as it was too hard to take care of.

Growing up I never knew the dangers I would later face when I would consistently change my hairstyle. At first it was at my mother's request, as she would do all these beautiful styles with my hair. Then it became something I held on to. Something I was afraid to stop.

It began with me never wanting to wear my hair natural in public. Of course, being young, my hair would always be out for the world to see, but as I got older the comments got nastier so I believed the narrative that I looked better with fake hair instead of my own. With that came lots of extensions, lots of money, and the biggest insecurity that I was always afraid to face.

I had this belief that if I had hair that looked like everyone else's, no one would be able to see who I was. I allowed my hair to define me, and I became chained down by this narrative that I would never belong if I didn't conform.

(I must say that I still do change my hairstyle, and put extensions in. This story isn't to say that people who decide to express themselves through their hair have self-love issues. But for me, I had to get to a place where I was no longer blinded by this so called 'perfect beauty'. When that took place, I could safely express myself while still loving the hair that I was born with).

Even though I knew I was heading down a dark path, I chose to ignore all the warning signs and carried forward without addressing any of the issues that were staring me right in the face. All my insecurities were coming to light, and I started asking myself the tough questions that were keeping me bound to this narrative of not being good enough. *Who am I? Why am I black? Why don't I look like anyone around me? Is there something wrong with me?* And my ultimate favourite, *Why can't I just be like everyone else?* These thoughts took control and left unwanted fear that was hard to replace.

I started looking for answers in all the wrong places, and let my mistakes take hold of my identity. It was like I was being held hostage by my own mind. I thought that in order to break free, I had to reject all of my characteristics and attributes as much as humanly possible. I believed that if I wanted to thrive in a white world, I had to be someone I wasn't. I adopted the belief that it was a burden to be black, and it pains me to say this, but the hate I had for myself got to the point where I did not like the colour of my skin.

I remember praying in my room, begging to be the same as everyone else, praying for that freedom, and praying for that peace. But deep down I knew that I could never change who I was born to be. It was in that moment my emotions led me down a dark path of destruction and self-hate.

The choices that followed led to a trajectory of my life that I never thought I would ever experience. I became someone I didn't even recognise, and I made decisions that I had thought I would never make. Every drink I had became a way to turn off the noise that was going on inside my head. The smoke I would inhale became an addictive external substance that allowed me to self-harm. The drugs that later followed were used as an escape from every problem, every decision, every unanswered question that I couldn't face. The men that would lie next to me were a cry for the attention that I so naively craved.

I became lost in the sea of people, trying to find my way back home even though at that point in my life, I had no idea where home was for me.

Searching outside of myself to find my truth led me to use these external sources that I later realised would never fill that void. I'd search for answers in friends, my community, drugs and alcohol, and I would always come up short. I'd put such high expectations on everyone around me, hoping that they would put back the pieces of me to the puzzle that I was so desperately trying to solve.

Maybe if I dressed like her I would feel better. Maybe if my hair was straight and silky, I would look like I belonged. Maybe if I acted like her, no one would notice how different I actually was.

There were a lot of what ifs and maybes swirling through my mind constantly. But it became a predictable formula, ending with me broken on the floor in the same place, with the same storyline. I understand that no one has a perfect life, we all have our ups and downs, and we all have different experiences that shape us and help us grow. But in these moments, each one taught me about a new part of myself without me even realising it. With every decision, every mistake and every lesson, pieces of me were starting to seep through, and my identity was starting to burst through to the surface.

Those moments, with every twist and turn, led me to where I am today.

Who knew that one day this persona would all come crashing down. No matter how far I ran, no matter how many times I would try to hide, no one and no place was going to feel like home. The longer I fought to reject myself, the longer it took for me to step into my truth.

When I would look at myself in the mirror, it was like a ghost was staring back. I wanted answers from my past to dictate who I would become, but every path I went down was a dead end. With each turn I was forced to repeat experiences over and over until I was ready to truly face what was going on.

That day I stared into the mirror, and I finally had the courage to admit what my actions had screamed at me for all these years. *I don't love you.*

When I took that first step I didn't expect the power of the emotional wave that would engulf me moving forward. I became angry, wanting to blame everyone around me for the way I was feeling.

But in the end, all I was left with was me, myself and I. With lots of moments of self-reflection, I finally could heal my perception of beauty, but more importantly I could heal my inner perception of myself. I no longer had to try to fit the mould, and I no longer had to be someone else's version of truth. I was finally seeking my own.

With each step, I became ready to uncover everything that made me, well, me. I went down a spiral of shame, and guilt, but with all that darkness, I eventually found the light. I was no longer holding on to my mistakes, and I was no longer carrying the weight of other people's opinions and words like they were my own. I opened my eyes wide, and behind all that hate, I could finally see the love that I had searched for my whole life.

Of course, it was not easy, in fact it was often painful. But when you're fighting for something, it's never a perfect journey. It's that endurance that pulls us through, and finally takes us to the place where we were always meant to be. Sometimes we may wanna give up, we become hopeless, think the journey is too much to handle. But when we turn to self-love, that is when our journey can begin, and that is where my journey truly began. I let go of damaging thoughts and patterns and stepped into vulnerability and strength. I started looking at life through the eyes of a child and allowed myself to experience any and all emotions that came up without fear or judgement. Finally, I allowed myself to come back to a place where I had a curious mind and a heart full of love.

Searching for those untold narratives within ourselves is an important part of life. Unravelling those stories helps us bring our highest vibration forward, and helps us live a life that is in true alignment with who we are.

The moment I was brave enough to sit in my darkness was the day I was finally free. I look at myself in the mirror now, and there is a new narrative playing.

I'm not saying that I don't have times where that old script takes hold and starts repeating old beliefs over and over again. But I now have the tools to help me navigate through those times, and I have the strength and the courage to fight back.

I finally stepped into my truth, and became empowered by my truth, so that I could live in my truth. Because let's face it the only person who can get me there is me.

# About the author

## Theanna Jordann

Theana Jordann was born in Limbe Haiti. She was adopted and brought to Canada at the age of sixteen months. Theana now lives on a beautiful island, and you can always find her near the ocean, or hiking in the forest with her family in tow. Her passion for the arts is what keeps her strong, and she believes in the art of storytelling and the power that it creates. This I Know Is True is her first publication.

@theana.jordann

# 14.

# The wound of love

## DR SARAH JANE PERRI

*Tell your friend that in his death, a part of you dies and goes
with him. Wherever he goes, you also go. He will not be alone.*
— Jiddu Krishnamurti

The wound of love.
The healing through pain.
The light past darkness.
The wholeness through parts.

I am writing this piece after returning home from *vipassana*, a ten-day silent meditation course. Another attempt of mine to connect with not only myself, but to something exceptionally larger than that. Consciousness. The creators. The universe. The laws of existence.

In my time I have always searched for and propelled myself into fascinations that have the opportunity for transformation and uprising, choosing to expand myself as opposed to life's circumstances undertaking this for me.

For the longest time I have been fascinated by death, by endings, by last breaths, by final goodbyes. By the cessation of the physical body as we believe it to be, but the continuation of the soul or spirit regardless of any substantial proof this occurs. By hearts disturbing and yearning, by literally sensing an aching pain in your own bones and pieces. One minute here, and the next nowhere to be felt, no life to be observed. The precious moment of transition, if you have ever witnessed it, is one of knowing the exact instant when life floats to the succeeding realm—you can pinpoint the precise second that just the shell remains, unfilled and unmoving, no longer the highly intricate machine of existence. Bygone the person you loved inside.

Where is it that we and our dear ones go? Why is it that with life must come death? What is the significance of it all? What is it that we leave in our shadows? What categorically, really matters? Time as a human construct that represents the changes, growths, transitions and eventually obliteration of our very own being. Also, the human journey, an experience of boundless privilege but also tremendous discomfort.

Something so incomprehensible, yet rationally our minds know and are certain of the inevitable truth. But to make sense of this reality, we must take a path that only grief and wallowing lead us down, that only deep loss, and inner turbulence can facilitate. That only the complete cracking open of our own actuality can bring into existence. There are diverse circumstances that perpetuate or somewhat relieve the trauma that follows, like age, suddenness, expectations, relationship dynamics, and unspoken or expressed words and actions. Possibly regrets, possibly respite, possibly both of the bitter and sweet tastes. Sometimes complicated by the connections we had or did not hold.

But regardless, there is nothing that can prepare you for the anguish that follows. Chasing, *hunting* our meaning and purpose, or even worse, no yearning or determination at all for substance. Endlessly sprinting on the hamster wheel. Relentlessly searching for more—doing more, buying more, in any attempt to fill the deepening voids within ourselves—to no avail. Emptiness, fear and certainty or a false sense of safety becoming what we attain instead of what our essence is here to do. Trapped in the contradictory ideas of 'one day' and 'live in the moment' or the infiltrated naivety of cruel things happening to 'them' or 'others' and thinking *That will never happen to me*. Ignorant to the fact that our time too will one day be up. That every moment, every inhale and exhale is revered. Not asking yourself who, if not you?

Grief is our way of knowing genuine love in this world. It is a duality of immense privilege and vast disadvantage. Yet, very much like life and death, it's an inescapable actuality of our human existence and experience. To know loss is to know the greatest gift of all. To know what it is like to have cracks or scars in the most profound part of you is to know what the refining and purifying of the soul signifies. Those who have not experienced grief will have missed out on creating the wisdoms and depths that come only as a product of things falling apart. It is imperative to recognise that grief is a journey. Not a place to halt.

I had never experienced someone close to me becoming extensively ill or passing away. My only real acquaintance with death or suffering as a consequence of death was simply in the movies that I watched, the books that I read and the handful of hospital visits and funerals that I attended, which only affected 'other' people. It had untouched me for so long, possibly reinforcing the invincibility of my perception that we have time. A falsehood that only intensified my belief of fairness in the game of life.

What took the most beating were my faith structures in what spirituality and the rules of the world were. To learn that bad things can and do happen to the best people. And that life can simply be just as punishing as it can be miraculous. Without ever getting closer to or understanding why, except for merely, why not?

I learnt that I was not special and that I had not escaped and would not escape the unavoidable. Like all of us. Despite being warned of death's predictability and expectedness, the shock still violently obstructs you. Gasping and grasping. The brain not able to comprehend the happenings before you.

Now, this is not to take away the beauty of the life experience or even death itself (although most are not frightened of passing itself but by the dying process). By the deterioration of what we know and the loss of those we care for beyond verbalisation, death appears to be final. It is definitely an ending. But like all finales, a beginning is born.

The smells, the sounds and the interrupted memories of conversations and visuals that somehow make a mess of the happenings. Instead of a free-flowing memory or recollections, there are only fragments, flashes. The replaying of flickers; you're attempting to distinguish fact from fiction, unsure of what is real. Almost uncanny in its representation of the soul's mirror at that very point in time. Shards. Parts. Broken bits. Pieces of me. Pieces of the ether. The cosmos.

Trauma does not get processed in the brain in an orderly and neat fashion. Not unlike a jigsaw puzzle, suffering becomes a muddle of images, corners and parts that may or may not belong where we think or thought. This is not a weakness of the human mind, but a strength of the heart.

Grief does not only exist in the end of a physical life. It is delivered in numerous ways when we feel as though we have suffered the loss of anything, be it a relationship, job or even how we expected something should happen or be. We can grieve our dreams. Our previous selves. Our future plans. Our philosophies. People who have not 'passed', but whose identity is no longer visible or able to be experienced. Limbo. The midpoint between living and finalisation. We can grieve anything that had meaning to us. The stronger the emotional charge, the greater the angst.

In Buddhism, there is emphasis placed upon non-attachment, as attachment is seen as the root cause of suffering. Nonetheless, just how one does not grow devoted to a loved one is a skill that I am yet to acquire. But then, would I rather experience misery than to never have felt tenderness at all? Yes.

It could be argued that there is no attachment in authentic ardour. No control. Zero expectations. Merely acceptance and release. I do acknowledge that things are dissimilar, that circumstances have and continuously will change. And that I will expand not only despite this but because of this.

We need pain and deep movement to ignite the soul to another profundity. This I know is true. Once an overwhelming loss occurs, your life becomes two parts. It is separated into who you were before, and who you become after. There is no sameness.

Does grief lessen in time? The shock fades away. The wondering if it was all a bad dream dwindles. Gladness can be experienced. But the sorrow itself? I am not so certain.

Many great truth seekers speak of the dark night of the soul. A spiritual crisis. A turning point. This was definitely mine. A shattering of everything I believed to be solid ground.

That place of limbo is exactly where my mum currently remains after suddenly sinking into a coma for months and acquiring brain damage from a rare autoimmune disease (acute demyelination encephalomyelitis) before eventually waking a different person. I was not prepared for this outcome.

If I am truthful with you, I supposed when she woke—if she woke—my mum would be the one on the other side. She was not. Our roles reversed rapidly and I became the one by her bedside. Parenting and nurturing her. Myself naively thinking that the hospital would be our most vast battle. In hindsight this was most likely a survival mechanism to get me through the extreme disturbance to my psyche. The testing of reflexes, the poking and prodding, the waiting, the sterility, the nights in bulky hospital chairs (attempting to get any form of rest), the constant beeping of machines, the endless tubes, the iridescent lights and the hospital odour that still remains with me to this day. Her screams and grimaces of pain I will never erase from my mind. Observing the desensitisation of the hospital staff, and the business reigning over human care and needs.

Yet, every so often a glimpse of hope in human form that had not yet been sucked in by the system and compassion remained, at least for now.

I remember thinking that this was not a place you would want to die. Removed from beauty, from nature, from care. From what makes us human. We are greatly detached from our roots.

This was the beginning of the loss of my greatest friend, family and confidant. Years on, the suffering continues relentlessly in ways that only those caring for loved ones with brain injuries could realise. Her eyes staring mindlessly into space. Voice carrying a higher pitch. Childlike nature now where the super adult that parented me once laid. The muddle in random phone calls. The same reassurances and conversations repeating, with no permanence. The lack of understanding of consequences and the unkindest of words that no longer get filtered. Watching the most self-determining person I knew become solely dependent.

The feeling of being alone in this world never felt so clear and convincing. I could sense that there was not another single soul on this earth that loved me unconditionally the way my mother did. And not another human ever would or could. I had never had a relationship with my father after he went absent when I was one. It seemed as though I lost both of my caregivers as my mum bore the responsibility of two roles. And I now was left parentless. Solitude in the cruellest form.

I was not new to the feelings of loneliness. I had been different and misunderstood ever since I could remember. But this seclusion touched differently. I had the privilege of assisting in the care of someone who cared for me, but was also undergoing constant emotional turmoil generated by woe for who and what was.

I have a birthday card from my mum that was gifted to me just four weeks prior to her loss of consciousness, the writing a representation of a moment in time that can never be again. The essence of her is in those handwritten words. At times I ring her mobile phone merely to listen to her voicemail. The speech I once knew and miss, the expressions I am so frightened of failing to recall as they increasingly began to fade from my mind each day. My brain is a constant fog and mist.

The most gentle and empathetic people in the world are that way for a reason. There is a reason the people who seem to have lost the most often discover more of their true selves than others in this world. It's because they have had to do so, over and over again, delving deeper with each wound. They begin to harvest the art form of relentlessness and even happiness. Of beauty that only unfathomable agonies can bring into being. The wounded healers of our generation. The scars being a representation of strength and the ability to rebuild, reminders not to forget our tenacity and magnificence.

My interpretation of death has expanded to include the ending of something far more intricate than the material body and the beginning of the next existence, but only when that world or the universe's innermost knowledge decides that it is your time. When finding peace, joy can also happen. Joy can happen once you decide and know that there simply is no other way. No other option. No other path meant to be. Or it would be. No method of controlling what is.

Now, this discovery can be immensely painful—affliction of the acutest core. To want to gain domination of what is and regulate the predestined is nothing short of foolishness. Yet we do attempt it with every single fibre. Our hands not only clinging but clenching tightly.

But there is weekly, daily, hourly, minute-by-minute, second-by-second grief that breathes on past the acceptance. Recognition does not equate to painlessness. Triggers happen unpredictably and harshly at any given time. Other periods, the exact same stimulus produces zero effect, making the journey all that more complex to navigate. I discovered this form of misery when experiencing recurrent pregnancy loss. The effects on my body, my emotional state, my heart, my friendships, my work, my finances, my relationships, my womanhood, my worth, my soul; nothing was unscathed. Nothing was untouchable. Nothing was effortless. Nothing was free of pain. Nothing was sacred.

I was to stay in my very own form of limbo for years whilst navigating the loss of five babies and myself and my marriage as I knew it. Seamlessly separating the strongest of partnerships with the deepest of wounds and personalised healing encounters at vastly opposing pace and complexity. Losing my fourth pregnancy whilst by my mum's lifeless side in the hospital is a memory undeniably arduous. Stuck between losing my mother and eluding my opportunity to become a mother. Timing that was both poignant and mind bending. Heart fracturing. Squandering me as I understood myself, the world as I believed it to exist, my life as I thought it would be. And ultimately the cost of appreciation for my body and being.

Love was replaced by anger. Frustration and the deepest hurt came with the sense of being condemned, judged and held responsible for the traumatic experiences. There must have been something that I was doing 'wrong'. I received unwarranted and unwanted advice from those who never walked or could imagine the path. My schedule consisted of endless appointments. Eastern and Western. Conflicting beliefs and opinions. An endless maze and gamble, never reaching the prize. Being left behind whilst others moved past me and by me, smoothly meeting the expectations of society and embodying motherhood effortlessly. Operations, countless tests and invasions, and more acquaintance with how children come to be than anyone should ever have to recognise. The exhaustion of advocating for yourself in a tertius sea of others. Just another case. Just another number. Just another shattered woman.

There comes a point in every journey though, when that life is no longer worth the existence. It cannot continue. In time and through inner work, the agony will sting less and you will be able to start learning from your experiences. You will be able to acknowledge and make some sense of them, even contradictorily be appreciative and thankful for them at times. When the smile on your face is no longer a forced falsehood, again you will begin to experience pleasure, sunshine when you were unable to remember how the warmth feels upon your face.

You had only known the storms and coldness of rain as the crumbling of your existence commenced. But now, an unfamiliar individual has been birthed into being. Where cracks once formed, deep grace exists. Your greatest transformation has come from your vastest aching. You are no longer bothered by small inconveniences. Forgiveness comes easily, compassion more frequently. Your focus is more directed, purpose more important. Time, or lack thereof, is continuously in the back of the mind. You choose resilience and strength because there is no other choice.

Evolution and upheaval. A metamorphosis from pain into authentic contentment. The realisation of the preciousness of the present. Never taking moments for granted. The expression of love no longer difficult, coming without hesitation. The doing without knowing the how. No regrets. Occasionally the fatigue of the riding of the waves rearing and roaring, but the innate knowing that this too shall pass creating the necessary energy to sail through and beyond. Flowing, not struggling despite the unyielding storm. Peace even in the turmoil. Tranquillity of knowing that what will happen will happen. What will be will be. And you will be all right no matter what.

It is vividly clear that I am changed. I am not the same person that I was, though people expected me to be. I think even I did. But I am not. I am not damaged. But I am different. It can be a secluded place to be, but also a progressive and enriching one.

I began to see that mothering could be achieved in various ways. Not just the typical way. That I was placed on this earth, with this circumstance. So how could it be? It couldn't. Or it would be.

I believe that I was put here to speak on behalf of others, to bring attention and kindness to the stigmatised, take care of those who cannot take care of themselves, help those with immense trauma to heal, nurture those who feel alone, and to be a light in the dim. To forge my own path fearlessly. Courageously. Conscientiously. To be myself in spite of the repercussions or lack of external approval. And to seek agreement only from within. To live a life that has substance. And to know, that whatever the outcomes, I, like you, am brave enough to meet them.

# About the author

# Dr Sarah Jane Perri

Dr Sarah Jane is a Network Spinal Chiropractor, Yoga and Meditation Teacher, Holistic Counsellor, Energy Facilitator and has an extensive interest in learning about world religions, eastern philosophy, culture, nature, animals, art, self-improvement, spirituality and ultimately living in alignment with her true purpose.

She is much loved by her clients for her empathy, kindness, ability to create genuine rapport and her boundless knowledge of the human experience and mind-body connection.

www.drsarahjanechiro.com
drsarahjaneperri@gmail.com
Instagram @en_light_n_drsarahjanechiro
Facebook @drsarahjanechiro

# 15.

# Honouring your true essence

## REBECCA RUSSELL

**How do we honour our true essence?**

The first thing we need to do is discover it. And we will discover and rediscover it time and time again throughout our lives. When you look at the cycles of nature, there are deaths and rebirths all around us. And we too are a part of nature. We too as women are cyclical beings.

We are ever evolving, shifting, changing, growing, shedding and rebirthing throughout our lives. There is never a time when we reach the final destination of who we are. It is dynamic and fluid. And this is why it is important for us not to attach ourselves or grip so tightly to who we once were, or who we thought we were going to be, but rather honour who we are now and who we are becoming.

When we are on the path to self-discovery, there is often a lot of unlearning and de-conditioning that needs to take place in order for us to peel back the layers of who we are and what we are here for. Our subconscious mind and patterns are formed before the time we have reached our eighth birthday. This means that from the time of our conception up until the age of seven, we are absorbing all of the patterns, stories, experiences and beliefs of our parents and those closest to us. Alongside this, we have the potential to inherit any traumas that our ancestors have experienced and take them on as our own in our physical and energetic bodies.

As you can see, there are a lot of potential contributing factors that can interfere with us honouring our true essence. So how can we connect to our true essence? By making time to connect to self each and every day. If we do not make the time to find stillness and connect to ourselves, how will we know what our true essence is or what it is that we want in our lives?

There are many ways we can tune in and connect to ourselves, and this will look different for all of us. What is most important is that you do what resonates most with you.

Some examples include:

- Practising yoga or similar mind-body practices
- Practising meditation
- Journaling—this is a great way for us to tap into our subconscious mind
- Doing things that bring you joy

Once you begin to prioritise making time for self-connection, and once you commit to making it a regular practice for you, you will come to know yourself better, and it will become easier to discern what is true for you and what isn't.

**How do we start to fully embody and live as our true selves?**
Once we have begun to discover who we truly are, we can think about what it is that we want in our lives and how we want our lives to look and feel. You might have some tangible goals you want to achieve. You might have a feeling that you really want to embody. And these

goals and dreams will often come through when we do the practices listed above that help us to connect to ourselves.

It is a common experience to still have some limiting beliefs about what is possible for us, and what we are capable of achieving, holding us back. But know this: if something is on your heart or in the vision of your third eye, it is meant for you, and it is possible for you. It is not random or pure chance, it is a part of your dharma (life's purpose). Of all of the dreams and all of the possibilities out there, your dreams have chosen to be expressed through you. And it is your life's work to honour them and bring them to life.

We as humans are infinite beings. We are limitless. And we are capable of achieving anything that our heart truly desires. And yet we place all of these barriers and limitations on ourselves that get in the way of us showing up as the best version of ourselves. Now is the time for us to be seen. Now is the time to give ourselves full permission to step into the light, to be the light, hold the light, embody our true essence and honour our greatness.

**How can we show up as our truest and highest version of ourselves?**
The place to start is to always trust our intuition. We as women are very intuitive beings. Your intuition might be communicated to you in a few different ways. Often you will feel it tangibly in your physical body. That drop in your stomach. That gut feeling. Your heart rate will elevate, or you will feel heat or energy in your body. These are all ways your body is communicating to you, guiding the way for you to take your next step forward.

Another beautiful way for you to connect with your intuition is to meditate on and bring your awareness to your Ajna (third eye) chakra—the space between your eyebrows. Our third eye is the energetic home of our intuition, and often our third eye is able to see things that our two physical eyes are blind to. Connect to your third eye, see the bigger picture, and ask yourself what it is that you need guidance on. If something doesn't feel right, it probably isn't.

Just as important as connecting with our third eye is connecting to and leading from our heart. Whenever you are in doubt, you can tune into your heart and ask yourself, *What would I do in this moment if I were to lead with love?* Our heart only knows love, our heart only wants what is best for all. If you lead from the heart, you will never be led astray.

**Be ok with being seen**

In order for us to fully step into our power and be seen and heard as our true selves, we need to get comfortable with being seen. Simply reading those words might make you cringe! There are so many of us who have felt the need to mask our true selves or show up as the version of ourselves that we think we 'should' be. We linger in the shadows where it is safe and familiar, watching everyone around us embody their true essence and achieve their goals and wishing that were us. But the truth is, that is available to you too. And it is your birthright to do so.

**Be ok with being different**

It is only natural for us to want to fit in with our peers, friends and family members. It gives us a sense of belonging and community. However, this often stifles our growth and blurs the lines of what is our truth and what is theirs. It is all too easy for us to go along with or agree with someone because it is easier than dealing with any potential conflict due to differing views. But again, this is not going to serve us and will ultimately lead to resentment and frustration.

While it is important to honour and respect others' points of view, it is equally important for us to own our voice and speak what is true for us.

Don't be led off the path of what's true for you, always remain in authenticity. This is when we need to get comfortable with being different and honouring our uniqueness.

## Don't play small in order to fit in

Have you ever felt the need to play down your achievements? Or worse, not even go after your dreams for fear of what others might think of you—for fear of suffering the consequences of tall-poppy syndrome, or others saying, *Who does she think she is?* or you saying to yourself, *Who do I think I am to actually go after the things I desire in my life?*

The truth is that it doesn't matter what others think about you or what you do with your life, as long as you aren't hurting anyone with your actions. And oftentimes when others comment on something in your life, they are projecting their own fears and insecurities onto you. Don't let the opinions of others skew your thoughts about yourself, or allow them to blur or dampen your vision.

Instead, you can lead by example. You can be an expander in the lives of those around you. You can lift up others as you walk the path that is true for you. And by doing so you will inspire others to do the same.

## Use others as inspiration, not imitation

We all have people in our lives we look up to, who we may or may not know personally—we might tell ourselves stories such as, *She has it so good/easy*, or *I wish I could have a life/business just like hers*. You might feel jealous or envious of what someone else has achieved. But the reality is that we don't see behind the veil of what that person's life looks like. We often don't see the years of hard work or the journey that they have taken to arrive where they are right now.

It is important to note that wishing for a life like someone else's is a futile pursuit, because each of us has our own dharma, our own unique purpose and calling in our life. And no one can live your life as you can. No one has the unique gifts and life experiences that you do.

Don't attempt to imitate someone else's truth. It won't work for you, and it certainly won't be sustainable for you.

We can be inspired by others, but we should never attempt to walk someone else's path.

### Move from a place of desire rather than obligation

How many times have you been motivated to do something because you thought you 'should' or because you felt a sense of obligation to someone? I think it is common, particularly for women, to feel like we need to be everything to everyone. We feel obligated to do things that we intrinsically feel misaligned to or simply do not want to do, and yet we force ourselves to do them anyway.

When we say yes to doing things that we wish to say no to, it feels forceful, it drains our energy and it builds resentment within us, both towards ourselves and towards the person or situation. And this is not supporting us to show up as the highest version of ourselves. This is not allowing us to fully embody our true essence.

Next time you are presented with a situation, invitation or offer, really take the time and space to sit with it. See how it feels in your body. If we tune into our heart and our gut, they will tell us the right decision to make. Of course, you can also factor logic into your decisions as well, asking yourself realistically whether you have the time, space or resources for this pursuit.

The other big factor we often face is feeling guilty for saying no because we want to honour the obligations we feel we have to another. And while it is absolutely a beautiful quality to be loyal and supportive to those in our lives, we should never do so to the detriment of ourselves. We can definitely be there to support others, but it needs to be because we genuinely want to and have the capacity to, and it also needs to be reciprocated. Because if you find yourself in a situation or relationship where there is an imbalance in reciprocity, this will lead to resentment and energetic depletion in the one who is always giving.

If you have decided, using the above steps, that a particular situation is not aligned for you, be open and honest with the other person and say that at this point in time you do not have the capacity to fulfil the task.

This is where we may need to put some loving boundaries in place in certain relationships or situations in our lives. This may not be an easy task for some, but it is a necessary one. People will respect you more for staying true to you and showing them what you consider acceptable and unacceptable behaviour, and where your energetic capacities lie. And if it is not received well by someone in your life, that in itself is a sign of misalignment, and perhaps you need to reconsider the relationship you have with them. We need to nurture our own energy first and foremost. If we allow our energy to be left unprotected and depleted, and we allow our boundaries to be blurred, we will be of no use to ourselves or anyone else around us, and we will not be able to honour our true essence.

**How to stay in alignment with your true essence when others don't agree with you or understand it**

We will all experience times in our lives when we are misunderstood, or simply not understood at all. And in particular, if you begin to evolve, change and grow, you are likely to experience this. Others will have become comfortable with how you once were. Perhaps they are comfortable with an inauthentic version of you, or a diluted version where you felt like you had to play small to fit in. But please do not allow this to stop you in your tracks on your way to stepping into your greatness.

We are here in this physical existence to learn lessons, to go through some potentially challenging or uncomfortable situations, and this might be one of those for you. But it is of the utmost importance that we continue on the way, that we continue to honour our true essence, no matter what. Because if someone is uncomfortable with your growth, your evolution, your awakening, that is their issue to deal with, not yours. Your growth has likely triggered something within themselves that is unresolved or untended to, and is being outwardly projected onto you. However, this is not your burden to bear. It is merely another lesson for you to learn from and solidify your commitment to honouring your true essence.

**Get comfortable with change**

Change, for the majority of us, is uncomfortable. It's unfamiliar. It challenges and stretches us out of our comfort zone. However, change is inevitable. It will come whether we welcome it or not. If this sounds familiar to you, I invite you to reframe this, to welcome change, to surrender to it.

There will be things, people and situations throughout your life that begin to feel out of alignment. They begin to feel like hard work. Or you simply feel that something isn't working anymore. So what should we do when this inevitably happens to us?

My advice is—don't force it. Don't waste any more time on it. It is not meant for you anymore. It is not supporting you to be the highest version of yourself.

We are in a constant state of evolution and flux, so it makes sense that things will naturally begin to fall away as we change and grow. And when they do, we allow them to with ease and grace.

When we release things that are no longer serving us, we create space for something new and more aligned to enter our field. We give ourselves the time and space to contemplate what it is that we now desire. What it is that we would like to manifest in our life. We give ourselves the opportunity to receive. We allow ourselves rebirth into the newest expression of ourselves.

Now that you have a good sense of how to honour your true essence, it's time to go out there and live and embody it! Consider this your permission slip (not that you ever needed one!) to step forward as the highest, most authentic version of yourself. Notice how things change for you. Notice how you feel when you really honour your true essence. Observe and practise gratitude for who you once were, who you are now, and who you are yet to be.

# About the author

# Rebecca Russell

Rebecca Russell is a wellbeing and soul connection coach and yoga teacher who supports women to connect to their authentic self through aligning mind, body and soul. Rebecca's methods are grounded in yoga practices, energy awareness and sacred rituals that support women to connect to self, feel vibrant and well, step into their light and own their purpose.

Rebecca supports women through two main avenues - single healing sessions and private 1:1 coaching that supports women to reach their wellbeing, spirituality, energy and self-connection goals.

**becrussell.com/private-coaching**
**Blog: becrussell.com/blog**
**Podcast: becrussell.com/podcast**

# 16.

# Cycles and ancestral connection

## LOREN HONEY

When I first heard someone describe menstrual cycles as 'potent not pollutant', I felt that deep within my bones as true. The connection between my menstrual blood and my ancestors started forming. I am a descendant of Māori and was born and raised in New Zealand, so connecting with this lineage has helped me feel more at home within my body and where I live.

And my cycle has been such a potent way of connecting with my ancestors and the land I live on.

There are many words used in te reo Māori (Māori language) to describe the menstrual cycle, and one of my favourites is te awa atua, which means 'the divine river'. In Māori worldview, it's believed that menstrual blood is a direct connection to the tūpuna (ancestors), right back through a woman's lineage, from her to her mother, her grandmother and all the way back to the atua (gods and goddesses), from which Māori believe we are all directly descended.

If our menstrual blood is a direct connection through our matrilineal lineage, then when a woman connects to her cycle and blood, she in turn connects to all her ancestors—right back to the atua. How can that not be healing on so many levels!

When my bleed arrives, I imagine my female ancestors gathering around me. I can sometimes almost hear their hushed whispers or ever so gently feel a slight wisp of air graze my neck, as though it's their breath. While we're menstruating, our hormones are their lowest and our aura is increased—some say auras expand ten times while bleeding. That makes sense to me, since this is when our senses tend to be heightened; we're more sensitive to bright lights and loud noises, and emotions can be triggered more easily.

This summer was the second time I'd been to the small island in Bay of Plenty where my tribe are from and the first time I went to our marae (tribal meeting house).

As my bare feet made contact with the land of my tribal marae, my period arrived. Waves of emotion gently washed through me as I considered the poetic timing of my womb blood arriving at the exact same moment I first stood at the meeting place of my ancestors. I had spent the last seven years learning as much as I could about menstrual cycles and had been fascinated with ancestral connection and healing. Add to that the hauntingly hard-to-put-into-words feelings I had always had around being Māori—but lacking the Indigenous knowledge or connection to our tribal land—and it all culminated into a day I'll never forget.

As a few tears welled up in my eyes and a lump formed in my throat as I stood on my tribal land for the first time, only one word came to mind. Tūrangawaewae (a place to stand, or more commonly, a place where one feels empowered or at home).

*I'm home*, I thought.

For the first time in thirty-five years, I felt a whole new level of what home feels like.

My sisters and I were welcomed onto the marae and the small group we were with gathered inside where the kaumātua (tribal

elder) showed us our ancestral lineage, handwritten on aged paper—
our ancestors all the way back to the waka that first arrived in New
Zealand over eight hundred years ago. We sat on the cream patterned
carpet listening to our kaumātua tell us stories of our ancestors and
how our tribe moved up the East Coast, eventually settling on the
lands we were then sitting on. We shared a meal and went on a tiki
tour around the island.

We went to the burial ground where my great-great-grandmother,
Hera, lay. The view from the urupa is glorious, looking over the sea
back to Mount Maunganui.

Listening to tales of our ancestors, I kept feeling tears well up
in my eyes. I finally was feeling the much deeper connection to my
Māori tribe, Ngāi Te Rangi, that I had been craving.

On the boat back to the mainland, I couldn't take my eyes off the
island my ancestors called home. I rubbed my belly, wondering what
my ancestors' bleeding rituals were. And how I could bring more of
that into my life.

The journey I had been on the previous seven years of decolonising
my cycle and reconnecting slowly with my ancestral lineage reached
a pinnacle on that warm summer's day. For years I had been learning
about our cycles as women and how potent, not pollutant, they are.
How our ancestors knew the magic of our cycles, our blood and the
gifts bleeding deliver.

I've been exploring the way modern society views cycles versus
pre-colonial society. And how by embracing my cycle I've also
reclaimed and begun healing my ancestral lineage.

Learning about and reclaiming ancestral heritage can be a daunting
task. For me, it's been beautiful—empowering while also bringing up
shame, tears and complex feelings. Sometimes I've wanted to throw

my hands up in the air and give up. Other times I feel overwhelming pride in all the places my ancestors are from.

Reconnecting to ancestors, lineage and our wombs is an innately personal experience and there's a lot of differing opinions and thoughts on how to do this—what's appropriate, what's cultural appropriation, etc.—so it's my intention, by sharing my stories and thoughts, to maybe help someone else.

I grew up in the suburbs of Auckland, New Zealand, and while I've always known I have Māori in my blood, I don't look it. Physically, I appear to be a normal Caucasian, and since I didn't grow up on my tribal land or speak te reo Māori (aside from the few words here and there that most people from NZ know), I had a real sense of disconnect from my Indigenous roots. Having multiple different cultures and ethnicities coursing through our blood is pretty standard these days, yet we tend to be raised leaning on one side of our ancestry. For me, that was my Caucasian side.

My ancestors are from all over the world. Māori, Australian, English, with some Spanish, Irish, Scottish, Jews, Church of England—mischief makers, rebellious ones, some had traumatic lives, some were kind-hearted and some were not so nice. It can be overwhelming to imagine all these lives in history that ultimately make me the person I am today. Maybe you'll resonate, or maybe exploring your own ancestry feels light and easeful.

Knowing that I have both Indigenous blood as well as coloniser blood is a strange concept to reconcile within myself. It brings up a lot of mixed emotions and very different worldviews, yet here I am, a living, breathing combination of worlds collided. And this is where connecting with my cycle has played a big role in helping me to harmonise all these seemingly opposing worlds. To bring some Māori worldview, ritual and ceremony into my cycles in the modern-day Western society I find myself in. From the many conversations I've had with people over the years around this topic, I know I'm not the only one.

As I fell down the rabbit hole of learning about menstrual cycles and how magically powerful they are—as opposed to how we're brought up to see periods as a nuisance or something not to be spoken of—I found what I intuitively felt deep down in the ways my pre-colonial Māori ancestors thought about women's cycles. They knew cycles to be potent, powerful, a symbol of the ultimate potential power to bring new life.

I learnt that menstrual blood is holy and revered in many indigenous cultures. Māori believed our blood was sacred and would anoint warriors with menstrual blood for protection and extra strength before going into battle. When women were bleeding, they would go to a special place to rest with other women who were bleeding at the same time. There they would learn more about matrilineal wisdom, practise singing and karakia (prayers or incantations), and the men would prepare special meals for the women. Women and men were not separated, they could come and go as they pleased, but there was a recognition of the sacredness of the time when women were bleeding. Our ancestors knew that bleeding is a time of letting go, quite literally; our wombs are letting go of what they no longer need.

So this has become a part of my practice with my cycle; when I'm bleeding, I'll think of what I want to let go of and release, and imagine my womb supporting the letting-go process.

I imagine how much more nourished menstruating women might have felt pre-colonisation compared with in our modern world. Being able to go rest as much as you like while the rest of the community looks after the children and day-to-day things. Imagine being given meals prepared for you and being able to use the sacred time of bleeding to turn inward and be around other women also bleeding. Imagine learning more about matrilineal wisdom and having the time and space to listen to your inner wisdom and strengthen your intuition. There's a special kind of magic where my thoughts drift to while I imagine that.

There's a misconception that menstruating was viewed as impure or dirty, and from what I know so far, it seems this is largely because ethnographers recorded history through their Western worldview from their homelands of England, rather than through the depth of understanding of Indigenous worldview.

Bleeding, for me, is a ceremony in its own way. I follow my ancestors' lead and rest as much as I can. Some months that's much easier to do than others; our modern world involves lots of responsibilities and things we have to do, so sometimes resting lots isn't as available, and that's ok.

I try to treat my cycle as a way to honour myself and my body as much as possible. In the days approaching my bleed, I'll try to prepare some meals that I can easily reheat or make so I can spend more time resting instead of cooking. I'll meditate more, since in that part of my cycle I find my meditations to be more profound and transcendent. Scheduling less for when I'm bleeding and planning to be social and doing lots more when I'm ovulating and have more energy feels good for me.

Indigenous cultures knew the power and significance of a woman's menstrual blood and different cultures have various views, rites and rituals when a woman is bleeding. They knew that women who are in their bleeding years could become pregnant and create new life within, and what could be more powerful than that?

I became fascinated with the kinds of rituals and ceremonies different cultures have for menstruation, particularly the pre-colonial Māori beliefs. I spent hours and hours, weeks upon years poring over books, listening to podcasts, speaking with other Māori women to find out what my ancestors' ancient practices and rituals were. And the more I learnt about it all, the more I began having conversations with friends about what I was learning. Some were equally fascinated and I would share what I had learnt with them.

Women would share with me that they too felt disconnected from their lineage. I've had conversations with women who feel disconnected from their Indigenous roots. I've talked to the ones who grew up with a strong connection to their lineage, the ones who grew up speaking te reo Māori and knowing their tribal practices. I've heard from women who are of European descent and wish they had ancient rituals and ceremonies for menstruation and other rites of passage, as though that's only for Indigenous people (hint: that's not the case).

The thing is, there are so many ancient practices, rite-of-passage ceremonies and menstruation rituals from *all* cultures, countries and peoples. It just comes down to looking into what *your* ancestral lineages are and the practices that are yours to bring to life, should that be something you want. Talk to your family and find out where your family are from, go back as far as you can. Get out a big piece of A2 paper and create a family tree. Ask the women in your family what their experiences with their cycles are, ask your grandparents, and see how far back you can go. Then do some research online or at the library on what the old rites of passage were, the rituals and ceremonies. How menstruation was viewed by your ancestors.

There's a red thread that weaves through our matrilineal line, so follow your red thread, so to speak.

While there's a lot of intergenerational trauma that some believe is passed down, I also believe there are so many intergenerational gifts. Don't forget to claim these.


When the occupation of sacred land at Ihumātau, South Auckland, became headline news after an eviction notice was served to descendants of that land, it quickly became a very real example of modern-day colonialism. My social media feeds became alive with posts and updates about what was happening as more and more people went out to Ihumātau to support the mana whenua (tribal descendants of the land).

I felt the internal pull to go out to the land myself; it felt like my Māori ancestors were calling me there, despite it not being my specific tribal land. As soon as work finished for the day, I got in my car after the sun had set and battled my way through peak-hour traffic. I had heard of some peaceful protectors being arrested and there was a strong police presence. I felt tense, uneasy. I didn't know what to expect and thought there was a possibility I could be arrested, but that wasn't going to stop me. My period had arrived that morning and I couldn't help but wonder if that was a sign from my ancestors to go out to the land and support the cause of #landback.

I arrived at Ihumātau. I felt so tired after a long day of work, and I normally rest as much as I can while I'm bleeding, but my womb felt drawn to Ihumātau and so did my spirit.

It was a cold night, windy and a little rainy, and yet the air was alive with the sound of Māori songs. Some people were offering cups of warm tea, there were small bonfires for warmth and people were huddled around. Amongst a peaceful and passive protest to keep sacred land intact, instead of being desecrated for housing, I felt immense pride in how our people all came together in support of each other.

I found one of my friends in the crowd and we hugged then looked at each other. Her eyes reflected my own pride and acknowledgement that we were right where we needed to be, making our ancestors proud by looking after sacred land.

I went out to Ihumātau a few more times over the following few weeks until the need subsided while the government, tribes and development company were in discussions over what would happen next. Each time I was on the whenua of Ihumātau, I felt more and more connected to my Māori roots. It felt like such a pivotal moment for so many people, the way it brought us all together for a common cause; despite most of us being from different tribes around the country, here we all were. Together, laughing, singing, making sure everyone was fed and had a hot cup of tea to warm our bellies. I found myself having conversations there with strangers (who quickly felt like old friends) about our cycles and the way my connection with my cycle was helping me feel more connected to my ancestors. They would nod, earnestly agreeing and encouraged to do the same.

Land is something that's important to Indigenous people worldwide and, from what I know, Indigenous people protect and look after their land because they feel like they are simply looking after future generations, instead of considering it 'theirs'. Whenua is the Māori word for land and it's also the word we use for womb and placenta.

All things that sustain us and keep the lineage growing.

Our bodies are much wiser than we know. It might seem like a simple coincidence the way my blood seems to communicate with me like it did when I first went to my marae or when I arrived at Ihumātau. I feel it's my body's way of saying I'm on the right path. I'm where I belong, my tūrangawaewae. My standing place. My blood is the divine river that connects me to my ancestors and the land. With each cycle, I feel more connected and more whole.

I am my ancestors' wildest dreams

And so are you.

# About the author

## Loren Honey

Loren Honey is a qualified life coach, international breathwork facilitator and award-finalist author. Her ebook, Sacred Seasons, explores everything related to menstrual cycles and is hailed as a book for anyone who menstruates or those who love people who menstruate. Loren's work and words weave together menstrual cycles, ancestral lineage healing and indigenous Māori worldview with her trademark fierce vision of elevating others into their sovereignty.

Loren's personal journey over the last decade—from married co-founder of an event management business to wild woman reconnecting with her ancestral lineage via her cycle—has illuminated her work in the world today.

eBook: lorenhoney.com/shop/sacred-seasons
Offerings: lorenhoney.com/offerings

# 17.

# Gatherings

## REBECCA LEE

What better catalyst for change? A global pandemic, generating a sharp reminder that natural evolution can drag humanity to our knees at any moment. Masses of body bags on the capital-city streets of First World nations. None of us is immune from harm at any moment of time.

Is this pandemic environment not telling of the volatility of life? Such fragility exists, whilst we perceive the illusion that we have some control amongst the chaos of the world. With empathetic immersion, I feel the burdens and struggle of mankind, not bound to any race, culture, borders or religion. Boundless suffering is projected to us daily with the switching on of any media.

I didn't always process the world this way. A transition to motherhood has been more than just a death of my ego-centred mind. The decade of my twenties was egotistical. Filled with immaturity, a lack of stressors and excesses of time to prioritise any of my own needs. It was glorious. A freedom of kinds.

Motherhood has birthed extreme pressure and stress to deliver my children a reality free from harm—an unrealistic goal to surround them with constant safeguarding. It has caused the death of my own carefree and selfish existence. Changed the wiring of my intellectual system to be centred on the nurturing and protection of others.

I have been gifted the responsibility to nurture and protect two beautiful souls that still flourish in the innocence of childhood. Just the thought of those struggling with fertility reading of my battle fills me with immense guilt. For what greater treasure exists amongst such cruelty?

Yet it is the knowledge of evils that floods my mind and days with anxious focus. Abduction, assaults, warfare, famine, death, murder, ecological and natural disasters. Thoughts and worry about these kinds of events often hijack my ability to live with presence and soak up my children's laughter.

I don't want to sound ungrateful, but this life transition has dragged me to the utter depths of despair. I feel within me a deep sense of regret and failure for all the days I could not muster gratitude. The lost moments that should have been captured by celebrating the immense blessings my womb space has borne.

In truth, motherhood saw me spiral down—a sharp decline in mental health at what should have been the most joyous of times. The heaviness I have felt lay on my shoulders could be weighed in tons. New-found responsibilities exposed rocky foundations that had been built upon the wounds of my inner child.

Worry is a breeding ground for anxiety. For me, it's not just a restlessness of mind or the racing of irrational fear-based thoughts. It can be debilitating. My nervous system is overrun and fires off fierce pangs of exhausting endorphins that rob my body of the ability to leave my bed. Sometimes for days.

Anxiety attacks fiercely constrict the muscles in my body, so that when I finally drop down a level, those muscles feel battered and bruised. I lie in a foggy haze as I try to return to reality, as I wait for the fire in my neck and shoulders to extinguish so that I can once again lift my head and face the day.

These attacks were not always a common event for me, although I have always had an anxious ball of energy exist within my body. People have always known me to be a nervous fidgeter. My inner child was often exposed to the adrenaline that is released in flight-or-fight mode and I never recovered. I never developed the ability to control what is a natural stimulus engrained in our physiology for survival. I simply repressed it. Trauma can do that to people.

I have sound memory of the first time I had conscious thought that something was not right with my body. I was twenty-nine. It was an ordinary day working at the office, sitting in my ergonomic chair, with ergonomic office lighting. I was completely safe, highly educated and performing managerial functions in the peak of my career. Managing safety, quality and human resource systems. I had spent vast time and money developing my ability to identify, assess and control risk in all aspects of my employment. Up until that day, I had been able to manage the mental load. The only difference on this day was I had just found out I was pregnant.

The smallest of triggers occurred. My breath turned shallow, with my diaphragm hardly moving. I thought I was having a heart attack. Felt paralysed like a deer in headlights. I didn't know or understand what was happening, although some internal guidance system directed me to reach out to a health professional.

My first contact with a general practitioner left much to be desired. I tried to describe the things that felt not quite right in my body and some behaviours I was concerned about. The doctor was highly dismissive. They offered a spiel about mind over matter, that I simply had to decide to cease the habits and thinking I had described, then addressed the fact my pap smear was overdue. I felt unheard and spoken down to. I had to advocate for my right to access a psychologist through referral.

After a waiting period, I was eventually able to explore my mental health with a compassionate practitioner. I was finally offered clarity on what was occurring. A diagnosis of anxiety and panic attacks. I attended six sessions of cognitive behaviour therapy, developed a tool for management and was then sent back into the world, unsupported but with well wishes.

For some time, I was able to soothe my nervous system with the visualisation of a catastrophe scale. When I was feeling anxiety, I had been encouraged to contemplate a catastrophe scale of one to one hundred, then give a numeric value to where my fears genuinely sat. This served its purpose for a while. I plodded along, although lived with a feeling I would describe as balancing on a tightrope. I didn't even see the fall coming.

The birth of my second child and the slow breakdown of my relationship with my children's father fuelled a further decline in mental health. I didn't address it and continued on, internalising stressors and irrational fear-based responses. Pushing them down to go about life. But nature has a way of forcing them to the surface.

My nervousness and fidgeting habits evolved to something more sinister. Panic, fear and dread again escalated and I presented to the mental health system for a second time. This practitioner helped me develop understanding and educated me. What I had thought was just an inability to find stillness was actually self-harm and self-soothing tactics that had significantly progressed.

Body-focused repetitive behaviours fall into the family of impulse control disorders. They were my go-to for everyday release, performed in a trance-like state, as the negative thoughts churned in the background of my unconscious mind.

Trichotillomania is a hair-pulling disorder. I twirl the hair on the left-hand side of my head amongst my fingers, then rip it from my scalp in chunks. I do this every night as I try to soothe myself to sleep. I stopped attending a hairdresser some years ago, too embarrassed at the significant disparity of hair on my head.

Dermatophagia is a skin-picking disorder. I was ripping chunks of skin from the soles of my feet, making it painful to walk on occasion. I bite the skin surrounding my nails down to the first knuckle on each of my eight fingers and two thumbs, regularly leaving bleeding and stinging welts that then scar the skin.

My failures to address my mental health and anxiety had led to regression and the need for medication management. For the first time in my life, I started putting conscious thought into my mental health battle. I put significant consideration into the impact and toll it was having on my everyday life. How sources of unhappiness and the misalignment of values were fuelling my condition.

I birthed my anxiety from the shadows and started to make fierce assessment of my priorities and direction, awakened to the interrelation between conscious decision making and enabling greater sources of happiness and content to fill the days. I made some fierce choices. Decided to separate from my children's father, decided not to return to my previous career. Two of my biggest stress sources. I found within myself a reserve of strength and willpower to make these significant life changes. To prioritise my health and happiness above all other things.

With the breakdown of my relationship and guilt of separating my children's family, my anxiety was already at what I thought to be peak levels. Yet I felt completely confident in my decisions. I thought surely this was it for me. Felt my life being placed back on track with a sense of purpose. I naively thought I had regained some sense of 'control'.

In the middle of March 2020, I moved out of the home I owned and into a rental with my two children. Ready to take on the world.

Just days after rehoming myself and my children, a state of emergency was declared by the government in response to the growing coronavirus pandemic. There was a mass shutdown of industry and I lost my employment. Welfare lines ensued in all Australian towns as far as the eye could see. A vision likened to a great depression. Our society was forced to make personal sacrifices to stop the spread of the virus for community health, a greater good.

My personal sacrifice was being catapulted into a mental health crisis.

I had no access to my assets or money, which was frozen in joint bank accounts, awaiting settlement through legal proceedings. I had no source of income. The tool I had become so familiar with and reliant on, my catastrophe scale, was off the chart.

I didn't know how I was going to pay to keep a roof over my children's heads, started to worry about national food supply as panic buyers stripped supermarket shelves. We were forced to stay at home on government directives. I took on the role of primary school teacher with a shift to homeschooling, and just for added pressure was trying to absorb a barrage of information on how to protect my children from a virus that seemed to be decimating worldwide populations.

In that week, I lived through a progression of cataclysmic events. I felt a large scale and violent upheaval of my world, felt immense and imminent threats to the safety and welfare of my children.

I was forced to join the welfare line. Sat on the concrete sidewalk for half a day. By myself, in shame. Racing thoughts of survival for me and my children flooded me. I was awake but living a nightmare. I could barely breathe. Barely talk when I finally made it to the front of the queue. Holding back tears, I felt so close to breaking down. It was humiliating.

Once my application for welfare assistance had been made, I left and power walked straight to a doctor. I begged the receptionist to see somebody. They took me to a quiet part of the clinic, offered me water, and in hardly any time, led me to an open door with a gentle hand placed on my back. My fear and dread were so evident to every person that laid eyes on me.

I paced that room for nearly an hour. In panic, but finally in privacy and safety. I hyperventilated for so long. When I finally could draw breath and speak of all my burdens that day, the doctor gave me a contact number for admission to a mental health facility. Referrals were made to a psychiatrist and a psychologist, with warning it would likely be a long time until I could access those services. That was everything that could be offered.

I returned to my new home that I couldn't pay for and seriously contemplated that my mind did not have the ability to process this life event. It took hours for my breathing to return to normal. My face was swollen and my eyes itched from a steady stream of salted tears. I felt my soul visiting Death Valley. I felt my body and all its support systems malfunctioning.

On that day, I was delivered a crossroads. A forced choice. Do I make a phone call, allowing myself to succumb and be admitted to a mental health facility? Do I allow myself to completely drown, or do I continue to fight and do all that is within my power?

I chose survival.

I spent the next day contacting every person I could think of that I had built personal rapport with throughout my lifetime. I visited essential industries still operating in my town. I presented to offices, reception desks—asked strangers, *Do you have any work?* Data from the Australian Bureau of Statistics indicates nearly 600,000 Australians lost their jobs in April 2020. Somehow, in all that madness, I found not one job, but two. I was gifted a kindness, I was gifted opportunity.

I felt a return of gratitude for the little things. A roof over our heads, food on the table, running water, heating systems, healthy children.

Over the ensuing months, somewhere between the outcry of political mismanagement and wave of social narcissism, I saw individual efforts that upheld our humanity. Ordinary people, with similar battles, offering to share food. Pleading with people not to be too proud to reach out if in need. I witnessed people sharing social media posts telling people not to worry if there was no bread on the shelves; they knew how to bake at home and could deliver a loaf. I saw Spoonvilles pop up in my local town to return a sense community to our children's upheaved lives. Messages of hope and wishes to stay safe were painted on fences in bright colours. I received a letterbox drop requesting I place a teddy bear in my front window so that children could marvel on a bear hunt while out on a family walk (one of our few freedoms at that time). Walking was one of the few opportunities to leave the isolation of our homes without risk of persecution and financial penalty through our judicial system. It gives me immense pride to have witnessed such kindness and compassion from strangers.

Our existing social structures had been decimated. Parliamentary sittings were cancelled. Industries halted worldwide. Education systems closed. The doors to our social fabrics and religious gatherings had been cordoned off and locked. With this, we started to realise the importance of community. We learnt the value of scaffolding people around us in new and innovative ways.

By the time a state of disaster was also declared in August 2020, my brain had started to find calm. My fight-or-flight response was no longer being activated many times daily. This was not a result of interventions of the healthcare system. I was still on the waitlist to access mental health services.

The calming of my nervous system came about by spending those months connecting with kindred spirits. We were vulnerable in our online gatherings. A women's circle. We shared stories of our mental health challenges and struggles, our triggers, our body responses. We worked together on rebuilding the foundations with which we respond to events in life. We explored natural and alternative healing therapies and taught ourselves how to be more resilient. We scaffolded each other on this transformational journey.

I became adept at mapping the effects anxiety had on my body, developed the ability to articulate my conditions, how I struggle and the effects anxiety has on my life. I developed the confidence to start having conversations with my employer about the challenges I face with mental health and the ways I need support in a work environment to manage it.

I evolved to tune in to not just the thought-processing centre of my brain; I learnt to listen to my nervous system. I learnt to let important decisions not be made by just analysing thought, but through the messages delivered from a heart-centred space.

In celebrating awakened women, I celebrate all women who step into the shadows of their existence and explore the depths of their own pain. It is a celebration of uniqueness. These scars bear a story of individuality. From the scars, fear that has come to fruition binds us. It gives us a capacity for empathy, to connect with another human and help share burdens.

Our species evolves through lived experience. We advance through the lessons of adversity. I have learnt that I am not alone in the fears that my anxiety often causes me to overthink. My fears are a universal fear. Caregivers worldwide are all presented with the same affliction. How can I protect the ones I love? My truth is that I have learnt I cannot control the fear, but when those dreaded events do occur, and they will, people will gather around me.

We are engrained with a survival mode to protect that which we cherish. This pandemic event has helped us regain a sense of this universal love, extended the offering to assist in the protection and nurturing of our neighbours, our community, the next generation.

The truth is, we will never have control of our fear of chaos. However, in times of our greatest adversity, we can either choose to drown or we can choose to awaken.

# About the author

# Rebecca Lee

Amazon best-selling author, Rebecca Lee, has developed a sharp skill set of word mergement. Holding a bachelor's degree in business management, her profession requires report writing for an executive level audience. A boredom arose from this sterile, analytical writing genre which gave catalyst for creativity.

In recent years, Rebecca transitioned to crafting poetry utilising a dialect of mystical realism. Highly introverted, this Author finds writing to be the safest form of expression and communication. An outlet for processing, self-exploration, healing and transformation.

Connect with Rebecca Lee's writing, workshops and events:

www.rebeccaleeauthor.com

www.circleofconsciouscreation.com

*

# 18.

# This is my truth

## KAYLENE PARKINSON

My truth comes from knowing the space we live in is also occupied and entered by other energies. My truth has shown me that we are connected to a higher force that is gently stirring within us, guiding us to listen to our innate wisdom and supporting us to remember our life's purpose.

I can't unknow what I know, and I wouldn't want to, even though my younger self would disagree! My awakening has gifted me forty years of self-growth and enriched my life with insights that I'd be oblivious to if it weren't for my connections with spirit.

Spirit connection, for me, means the same thing as connecting to the universe, God, higher source, my truth, divine light, inner knowing/being, the creator—it's all one and the same.

The first three decades of my life, there were times that I was scared of my awareness of another realm entering Earth's dimension. At times I wondered if I was a beacon for energies; did they know that I was able to sense them—or was it just that I was sensitive to their energies and could feel when they were near?

My earliest memory of spirit began with the voice nobody owned.

I was four years old and annoyed. Night after night I would hear my name being called. *Kaylene.*

I'd ask, 'Who is it and what do you want?'

The reply was always, *Come here.*

I remember that I wasn't afraid of the voice, just annoyed. I wanted them to tell me what they wanted and to stop calling me.

I would tiptoe down the hallway to see who was calling my name.

I would tell my parents I could hear someone calling me and they'd say, 'Back to bed—no one's calling your name.'

Frustrated from the same events night after night, I started to sleep with a pillow over my head in an attempt to muffle their voice and fall asleep.

Eventually they stopped …

We moved to our next house when I was nine. This house had a heavy energy. I often felt like I was being watched.

Odd things happened in the middle of the night, like the time I was thinking about how Elvis Presley died and suddenly my radio turned on by itself and played church bells. My youngest brother once saw a mother with two young children standing in his doorway. Most nights I would hear the sound of someone walking up the stairs; I would burrow under my covers to try to block them out. Occasionally I was brave enough to walk down to the landing with my hockey stick in an attempt to confront my fears.

My parents sold this house just before my fourteenth birthday. My cousin later told me she knew the family that moved into the house. They hated living in it after they saw the doors of the kitchen cupboards opening and shutting by themselves!

I'm so thankful I never witnessed that type of activity!

I like to think that the spirits of that house enjoyed my family living there. Maybe they weren't happy when we left, so that's why they acted out.

When I was twenty-one, my outlook on life changed forever when I saw a ghost for the first time.

In a deep sleep, I was dreaming my best friend's brother was being chased. My soul was pulling me out of my dream; there was an alarming need for me to wake up. I was so startled by this sense of urgency that I sat up, only to become even more startled because there was an old lady leaning over my bed. Her sweatshirt was green and her hair was grey and overgrown.

I screamed at this intruder, but she stayed still, oblivious to my high-pitched scream.

Then I noticed she wasn't solid. Terrified, I screamed again and watched as she gradually dissipated from her head down.

I had seen with my eyes into a realm I always sensed existed, and I didn't like it!

It had scared me so much, I needed to sleep with the light on in the hallway for a few weeks following.

Spirit had insisted I see this. They had woken me so I could see.

I remember being worried about the meaning of it all. The urgency to come out of my dream, wake up and see this ghost.

From an increased awareness grew a deep curiosity, guiding me to understand more about this strange, unsettling truth, to ponder over the world we live in, knowing there was so much more to it.

This perspective was my place of daydreams. A space of contrast: I was scared to see more but at the same time had an urge to allow my conscious awareness to grow and understand.

Wanting to know more. Scared to know more.

Ironically, my fear was keeping me from connecting to the higher vibrations that were waiting patiently for me to acknowledge them. It took me a few more years to acknowledge source energy before I could transition completely out of fear and into an enlightened perspective.

In the third decade of my life, I experienced some of the most terrifying nights of my life when I experienced psychic attack, medically known as sleep paralysis.

The symptoms are described as being awake, or waking up, but being unable to move a muscle or utter a sound whilst experiencing hallucinations in which the person feels or sees the presence of an evil and threatening individual.

Tick to all of the above ... except the hallucinations.

I was terrified of the spirit realm. I wanted to know how to stop this from continuing.

I couldn't tell a doctor. I knew the questions they would ask. *Have you heard voices before?* then the next question, *Have you ever seen things that aren't there?* A referral to a psychologist and most likely medication would have been the prescribed answer.

Most of my life I'd been scared of entities invading my space; now I was physically experiencing my body being pushed down by the unseen while I was in my bed, paralysed, unable to make any sound or move a muscle.

I was terrified of the possibility that an energy was trying to possess me.

I lay in bed on high alert every night.

I felt like I was being haunted.

My parents and husband knew I was afraid but I never shared my deep fears. I knew no one who was able to understand what I experienced.

Social media didn't exist at this time—no Google, just a whole lot of stigma and judgement attached to clairvoyance. The books I found in the library were about religion and the paranormal … not a rabbit hole I wanted to go down. In hindsight, I'm grateful for the lack of information, the internet would have only served to create more fear.

Psychic attack led me to discover the power we hold when we step out of fear and take control.

One night, unable to make a sound, I repeated these words inside my head with conviction: *I am surrounded in white light. Only those from the highest of energy are allowed to enter my space. You are not welcome—you must leave now.*

To my relief, my body quickly came out of paralysis.

Negative energy has a dense vibration. The moment it arrived, the house would expand and creak, next the hallway door would click, and then immediately it would be in my bedroom beside me.

The following nights, when they tried again, I immediately began repeating my mantra from the first sound of the house creaking.

This ended the unwelcome visits and I got back to restful night sleeping. Happy nights!

From my early years, I sensed I had protectors, guardian angels. But I had become fearful of this realm, never wanting to connect with them, frightened to pay them attention in case they would show themselves to me. And afraid of other energies that could come.

But my inner faith was stronger than my fear, and so when I was desperate, I found myself instinctively calling for them to save me from drowning, and again to save me from the negative energies when I was terrified, lying in my bed, feeling helpless and vulnerable to the unknown.

Calling on spirit when in despair, I was answered immediately.

This is what cracked me open to the realisation that spirit isn't a force to be feared but a love that only serves to support.

Fear not only kept me from connecting to the higher realms but also kept a large part of myself suppressed because I was scared of failing.

When I was twenty-two, I was on a hairdressing workshop in London and was shoulder-tapped by world-renowned hairdresser Guy Kremer to work for him. I said I'd be in touch, but I never did because I was afraid I wouldn't be good enough. *All's good with where you're at*, I told myself. I just let fear step right in and squash any thoughts of excitement for an incredible once-in-a-lifetime opportunity. OMG, fear is the worst! #lifelessons

Fear will trick us into thinking we are keeping ourselves safe. It can encourage us to stay small as it effortlessly glides forward to take the controls, making us doubt our strengths and suppress our voice.

Unless fear is presented to keep us physically safe from harm, it's not serving our highest good. A space of comfort can prevent us from living life to the full.

I also try to let go of what other people will think. Worrying about what others may think quickly puts the brakes on being in flow!

Of course, I definitely still feel fear, but I'm no longer living my life in a space of staying comfortable. I remind myself to connect to my future self and see how she feels if I close the door on the new and unfamiliar.

Do I step into this new learning with all the failures and successes it may bring? This question pushes me to move forward; it reminds me that I am here in this lifetime to live to my highest good.

I make a lot of decisions through my intuition. It's always the decisions that test my comfort levels that I really want to make, and if I'm hesitant, my intuition nags me until I say yes. I've learnt that if I say no, I'll wonder *What if*, so these are the decisions I now trust my inner wisdom and say yes to!

We are raising our three children in an open space of awakened awareness. We speak easily and often about angels, source energy, energetic vibrations, intuition, guides, the energies of essential oils and crystal energy. If negative energy does show up, they know how to call in their protectors. My intention has always been for them to feel comfortable on their awakening journey as it unfolds.

Holding a belief that the mainstream masses consider to be unbelievable, unfathomable—psychotic even—is an interesting space to be in. We live in a culture where there is a constant need to judge and undermine.

When conversations about clairvoyance come up, people generally are pessimistic. I always feel called to say, *Hey it's the truth. Obviously, there are frauds, but the truth is we all have the ability to communicate with the spiritual dimension and those energies are able to come here … And your intuition—well, that's source energy, which is a part of each of us!*

Honestly it's often been a conversation I would prefer not to participate in … the sceptical questions: *I didn't know you were spiritual—How long have you been into that!*

And then there's, *I'm sure you believe what you say ... but in reality it's your imagination!*

Oh, and the blatant eye rolls aren't lost on me either!

Other times, it raises my vibration; I speak fearlessly and excitedly to those who are also beginning to awaken as they connect to the truth of this awareness and the insights of seeing life in an enlightened way.

I understand why people are sceptical; seeing and experiencing the unseen is beyond comprehension. Even I find it bizarre! I often wonder, *Why? How? What's the meaning of this?*

People's disbelief in clairvoyance doesn't make my experiences of knowing unjustified; it makes them even more sacred to hold. They are my truth.

In recent years I have developed a much deeper connection with spirit.

One night I was reflecting on how it felt like I was just going through the motions, ticking all the boxes of being a mum, wife and hairdresser. There didn't seem to be much else outside of my hats and I wasn't sure that was going to change any time soon.

Acknowledging these feelings led me to write to spirit ...

> I'm ready for more in my life.
> I'm no longer afraid. Please show yourselves to me.
> Show me what it is that I've forgotten.

I rolled the paper up, bound it with string, and placed it beside a photo of my nana on my altar.

My letter to the universe not only manifested in the near future, but also showed me the most extraordinary things.

One afternoon I walked out of my bedroom to witness something incredible.

Six feet in front of me was a spiralling vortex, made up of something I can only describe as energy. It was neither air nor water—yet moving fluidly as though it was. Clear and luminous, a beautiful, glistening, unearthly force of movement.

It was about one metre above the ground and 1.3 metres high, one metre wide at the base, narrowing towards the top.

I stood still, in awe of the moment, wanting it to last as long as possible.

In the tranquillity of this mesmerising experience, a shift happened—my core connection to source immediately deepened.

The energy formation stayed in the room for about sixty seconds before disappearing.

Seeing the metaphysical with my physical eyes left me feeling excited and confused. I wanted to know what it meant, what was the meaning?

This is the logical brain at work ... how, why, what.

I had forgotten the words I wrote only a few months earlier when I asked source to show itself to me and show me what it was I'd forgotten, and said I was ready for change in my life.

Six months later, I was in my bathroom when a bottle of frankincense essential oil flung itself off an open glass shelf and levitated two metres across the bathroom towards me. It dropped to the tiled floor without breaking.

I saw this with my own eyes. The bottle left the shelf and moved across the room.

When I write these words, I know it sounds bizarre. If someone told me they had seen this, I would also struggle to grasp it. It was dramatic, yet oddly this was a calm moment. It wasn't scary.

I'm the type of person who closes their eyes and covers their ears when something scary happens in a movie, so I was surprised I had no feelings of being frightened.

Spirit presented this to me as a sign; it was a positive experience.

My thoughts were a medley of, *WTF. This world is so incredible. Why is spirit going to so much effort to present to me in this dramatic way?*

At this point, maybe you're wondering if I take drugs; was I under the influence of alcohol, or was I sleepwalking? Fair call—but the answer is a definite NO. I'm completely healthy, no prescribed medications. I have very good health and wellbeing.

The explanation is one that can't be explained by science. It is in the realm of the metaphysical.

Twelve months later, in a dream I was shown six different branding images. I saw myself point to the bottom one and say, *It's this one.* It was an amethyst crystal.

In the morning, I shared with my husband that I had been shown logo images. I didn't know what it was to do with, but my husband and I both laughed and I knew I was going to be doing something with crystals.

Three months later, my nana came to me. She showed me visions of myself stirring large pots and she said everything was going to work out, that she would take care of the dynamics in the house while I did what served my purpose.

In that moment, I knew that I was going to begin making crystal intention candles. The visions I saw of the pots were me stirring fragrances into large wax melters; this is where the frankincense that spirit flung across the room fitted in.

Weeks later, the name LightSeed came to me. The name was a perfect fit; this idea had been a seed that was sown from the guidance of Light.

Next, spirit gave me the ideas of the names and their meanings, their fragrance blends, and aligned crystals and affirmations to go with each candle.

During the six months that it took to bring them from conception to birth, I'd get random energetic tingles of excitement. It was this energy that encouraged me to end my career as a hairdresser and step fully into the new business.

Spirit had directed me into a soulful business that I feel truly aligned with. It encourages me to walk in my truth and brings new learnings and connections.

I now connect to source energy every day. It helps me centre and assists with decisions and encourages me to live the best version of my life. Spirit has shown me the power of manifestation and it feels like a magical tool I have in my toolbox.

I'm always in wonder of the mystique of it all.

At certain times in writing this chapter, I have suddenly felt vulnerable; a heat of energy quickly moves from the pit of my stomach through my chest and expands to tighten in my throat.

A sensation of fear around sharing my sacred truths.

I'm sharing my truth to add body to the awakened collective, to raise conscious awareness and normalise what you may be witnessing on your awakening journey.

I encourage you to travel with confidence and sovereignty.

The knowledge I hold isn't from words I have read in books. It doesn't come from teachings of inherited beliefs. My knowing is firsthand and direct, constantly evolving and expanding.

My truth is in knowing we are all one, created from the same energy that creates every thing in the multi universe ...

My truth is a part of who I am.

It's in the ghost leaning over my bed. The lady walking towards me at Lake Pegasus. And it's the little girl standing beside my bed, looking sweetly at me with her long brown hair neatly braided into plaits.

The synchronicities.

The guidance the universe provides.

The orbs of light that bounced around my bedroom wall, telepathically telling me I was pregnant as I saw photographs in my mind's eye of a newborn baby.

It's in knowing something before it happens, with no logical way of knowing it to be true. Yet it is.

This is my truth, beautiful and cherished.

# About the author

# Kaylene Parkinson

Kaylene lives in New Zealand, she is a mother, wife, creator, and lover of all things mystical. She's an intuitive empath and source channel, born with an innate sense of awareness of the metaphysical.

Kaylene was honoured to receive trust from thousands of women for over twenty years as she assisted to invoke their inner goddess during her career as a hairstylist. Kaylene transformed women's hair with colour and cuts to suit their personalities and lifestyles, whilst holding space for many sacred conversations, until The Universe intervened in 2020 and gave her clear guidance to change direction and learn the art of a chandler. Following this guidance, she birthed a line of crystal intention candles with the intention of empowering others to awaken their inner wisdom and radiate positive vibrations through regular moments of self-care.

Sharing her magick with you! 10% off any LightSeed product, use code THISIKNOWISTRUE at www.lightseed.co.nz where you'll find handmade candles and more information and insights about fragrance, self-care, rituals and living life intuitively.

**instagram @lightseednz**
**facebook @lightseed**

# Sunsets

*As the Sun sets ...*
*We find stillness and continue to dream and breathe with the*
*Ancestors*
*and Journey home to heart, soul, spirit.*
*We weave together the Dreaming of peace, love and hope*
*to start a new day, a new beginning, a new future.*

— Annabelle Sharman

CPSIA information can be obtained
at www.ICGtesting.com
Printed in the USA
BVHW071751191021
619300BV00008B/143

9 780645 088748